August 1972
To Lester and Arlene Mindus
with fondest good wishes
and love
Leora Rubin

HowTo Defend Yourself at Auctions

By Leona Rubin

Westover
Publishing Company

A Media General Publication, Richmond, Virginia

SBN 0-87858-018-2

Illustrations by T. F. Hale

CONTENTS

For Simon

FOREWORD

Mr. and Mrs. Farbleheuter carefully used all four keys to lock their apartment door, found a taxi after only half an hour of jumping up and down the curb, and soon were packed cosily in an elevator on their way to the household-goods department of a large downtown store. (It happened to be an express elevator and they had to go down and start all over, but no matter.)

They shopped all afternoon, up and down escalators, back and forth across streets whose lights always turned red at their approach. In each store a salesman waited to appear until the Farbleheuters had had plenty of time to wander around making sure they were in the right department and then he brought out the few requested items. Everything was marked with coded information and a definite price, take it or leave it.

As the day wore on, Mr. and Mrs. Farbleheuter got more tired and more dispirited, oppressed by a feeling of alienation from the crowds of rushing people. They ended up taking whatever was shown them next, just to get through with it.

While they were unlocking the four locks on their apartment door, their neighbors, the Brackstonapples, clattered up to their own door just opposite. The Brackstonapples were also be-bundled, but smiling and excited, having a great old time and obviously very pleased with themselves. The drooping Farbleheuters watched them. "Hi!" burbled their neighbors, who had only moved in last week and no more than nodded politely till now. "Come on in and see this! You have to hear about this."

If you've figured out that the Brackstonapples had been at an auction, had an interesting, exciting time and got a couple of great bargains, not to mention an unidentified but absolutely antique object which they knew would be decoratively useful as soon as they worked out their ideas, you would be absolutely right.

There's something about auctions that puts a gleam in the eye and a rose on the cheek. Maybe it's that investing in antiques and objets d'art can be a wiser financial course than the stock market; or maybe it's the pleasure and pride of owning unique work of beautiful craftsmanship; perhaps it's the satisfied glow that comes with getting a good bargain. Whatever each one's reason, there are proved aesthetic and practical advantages to buying at auctions — IF you know what you're doing.

The key is the IF, because it's also possible to get skinned. To save you some of the pain and expense of finding out by experience, what follows will be the ins and outs of auctions for the average non-expert, non-millionaire who would just like to have some handsome things at the best possible price, and to have a good time acquiring them. Auctions are entertainment without buying a ticket — and the more you know about the nuances of what's going on, the better the show. Auctions are both small and big business, and a knowledge of how they work can mean money in your pocket.

The *Great Buy* is the dream chased by every searcher for antiques, objets d'art, fine things, and even ordinary articles. The *Great Buys* can be sought in little shops whose owners get much of their merchandise at auctions. But it stands to reason that the amateur who buys at an auction has to come out ahead of the professional dealer, because the dealer has to make a profit to stay in business, and his mark-up is usually from 100% to 200%. Thus, the epitome of the *Great Buy*, the sportsman's true test, is at the auction.

We'll skip admiringly but hopelessly over the best known auctions, those famous sales where hundreds of thousands of dollars are flung about with abandon. The bailiwick for the average buyer is the everyday auction held in a great variety of surroundings.

Leona Rubin
New Bedford, Mass.

3

. . . a lady described her reaction to her husband chasing down the old bottles he liked at auctions. "I encourage it," she said. "It keeps him out of mischief and is cheaper than golf. And he has something to show for his money."

1

AUCTIONRY FOR BEGINNERS

Buying at auction is a centuries-old means of exchange. The word "bid" was used by the Greek historian Herodotus when he wrote about his visit to Babylon in 550 B.C. and made reference to a comely maiden consignment.

The Romans held auctions right on the battlefield, after the dust settled. Their word for the sale of their booty was *auctionem* (sales by the increase of bids).

Though auctions have ancient historical roots, they haven't changed much over the years. They still offer the best combination of theater and suspense. Auctions are full of drama, excitement, and entertainment — in spurts, of course, or bidders and the auctioneer himself would be continual candidates for tranquilizers. To enjoy an auction between dramas you need patience. If you get restless quickly, wander in and out, you may miss out on the object of the century.

What is an auction?

The textbook definition of an auction would run
something like this: A gathering at which sellers put
up goods for sale, and would-be buyers are invited
to bid in competition with one another for the
right to acquire the property. Informally, an auction
could be called the greatest floating crap game
in the world. Professionals say it's the most
fascinating, competitive, tricky way of buying there
is. If you know what you're doing, there's no
other way to buy; and if you don't know what
you're doing, you can get nicked, diddled,
gammoned, and possibly hoodwinked.

Auctions can be recreation. In the early part of this
century, a lady described her reaction to her
husband chasing down the old bottles he liked at
auctions. "I encourage it," she said. "It keeps
him out of mischief and is cheaper than golf. And
he has something to show for his money."

Auctions are also like journeys, where expectation
is half the pleasure and the after-gloat, or at
least the recollections can provide endless hours of
conversation about the one you got or the one
that got away.

The code words

Auctions by nature are public occasions, but often
they're thought of as glamorous and mysterious
just because they have their own special vocabulary.
To dispel that fog forthwith, here's a short description of the most common terms. The fellow
who starts the auction process in motion is the one
who wants to sell, the *consignor*. The auction
house he chooses to act as his salesman then places

an *estimate* on his goods. The estimate is at best
an educated guess and whether it is an accurate one
substantially depends on a number of things,
particularly on how many people are interested in
buying. A *lot* is the number of pieces sold as a unit,
such as a set of china or a matched pair of lamps.
The *price* is what the item ultimately sells for—how
much one person at that moment is willing to pay
for that specific object. (Thus a few hot bidders can
make a monkey out of the estimator—albeit a happy
one; or an unexplainable slump in the bidding can
make the item almost a giveaway).

Knocked-down is auctionese for sold. *As is* means
the auctioneer disavows responsibility for chips,
cracks, wobbles or any decomposure that has set
in. *Buyer's privilege* gives the winning bidder on
one object from a group the opportunity to buy
the rest at the same price before they're put up
for bids. A *reserve* (also called a *starting bid*) is
the lowest price for an article the consignor is willing
to accept and is ordinarily used for high-priced
objects only. A *book-bid* or *order-bid* is a bid
left with the auctioneer in advance, stating the
maximum an absent buyer is willing to pay.
Provenance is a list of all the owners of a work of
art and where it has been exhibited and written
about.

Two bad words are *planting* and *shill*. *Planting*
is trying to conceal inferior pieces by mixing them
with valuable ones. A *shill* is another kind of sly
plant, an employee disguised as one of the bidders
to work prices up, acting on the same shoddy
principle that his frontier counterpart did in the
medicine man's wagon. These and other nefarious
practices that we'll go into later are disdained
by reputable auction houses.

Are auctions for millionaires?

About a handful of auctions a year sell items that are far and away too expensive for all but the very rich and institutions, such as museums and historical foundations. But consider that there are approximately 25,000 auctioneers in this country (double that if you include part-time practitioners) plus about 2,000 auction houses, and uncounted halls, barns, tents, and other temporary set-ups. Actually there are very rare exceptions to the 'everybody welcome' flag that flies the day of the auction. Spectacular sales for astronomic sums may capture the headlines, but auctions really constitute a medium-priced business that attract the widest kind of audience, including "just folks." There's no reason not to go to even fancy auctions. All those things come from homes of people of widely varying means and taste, and nobody lives with elegant things only. There might be beautiful paintings along with a wreck of an old upholstered chair. Auction sales usually combine things from various estates so there's something for everyone. Parke-Bernet, America's most famous auction house (now Sotheby, Parke-Bernet, of New York, London, Houston, Denver and Los Angeles) advertises "You are cordially invited . . . come by and join in the excitement."

There are all kinds of auctions

The very best auction galleries generally own nothing. They carry absolutely no stock of their own; everything is taken on consignment and the consignor pays their fee. There are auction houses in Chicago and New Orleans and Philadelphia and dozens of other cities who say "We don't want to retail," or "We're strictly agents for the owners." But the exceptions are in the majority— most galleries some time or other have to buy estates or works of art on their own.

Some auction houses accept nothing that is not an antique (and often *anything* that is) except from complete estates where they have no choice. Even good galleries have their minor days, particularly off-season, when they auction off odds and ends, or small estate lots, which they call "residual objects."

There are, of course, cheesy auctions, where every kind of junk under the sun, new and old, is sold. Some of them are regular weekly events— meeting places where people mill around catching up on the latest community news while being entertained by the auctioneer's jokes (corny but always appreciated). These affairs usually sport "character" types who come for the laughs and put on a bit of an act themselves now and then.

Between these opposites are the auction houses that sell fine things but dispense with the formality of the city. These have a nice relaxed attitude, without the haphazardness of the country yard or traveling auction. Operating in a properly set up gallery (no makeshift quarters), generally with catalogues, they have all the facilities to protect valuable merchandise. In the summer, some of them put up gala tents, which supply the summer atmosphere people like and extra space. Certain ones sell only fine art and antiques, but a glance at their catalogues would prove their contention that they're not too expensive for people like us—not even the annual special events, like the Oriental Auction on Cape Cod around which many devotees plan their vacations. Other such galleries sell household items and every other inanimate object known to man.

Catalogues and advertising

Auctions occasionally stipulate "Attendance to Sale by Catalogue Only." Sometimes an admission fee is charged which includes the price of a catalogue or is credited to purchases; in rare instances an auction house may advertise "apply to galleries for sales admission card." But the majority of auctions are open free to all.

Catalogues carefully combine reasonable accuracy with allure. They tactfully point out defects, such as "some repairs and imperfections," "some discoloration," "small chips," etc.

Catalogues sell for from 50¢ to $6. (They often cost more to produce—up to $25—but the galleries consider that part of their business expense.) If you don't want to buy one, they are available for reference at the exhibition. Presale estimates are frequently also available on request. "These," they stipulate, "are the Gallery's approximate valuations and should not be misconstrued as 'prices.'" Estimates are figured this way: if something should bring between $100 and $150, the estimate will read $125, and is usually a conservative guess.

The most common way of advertising auctions is in local newspapers or, for special sales, magazines and newspapers all over the country. A good auction house is willing to advertise and describe the goods so those interested in something will come (this is part of how they get consignments).

Much direct mail advertising is used—without exception they'll be happy to add your name to their mailing list—and there are posters, flyers, oral announcements at nearby sales, and finally the red flag out on sale day. You'd be surprised at how much mail order business the better auction houses do by catalogue all over the country, and even abroad. Parke-Bernet says 20% of their business is done by mail. Advertising brings not only people who need something, but those who can't bear to think what they might be missing.

When auctions are held

Of course, one can't just decide, "today I'm going to an auction." They have to be watched for. Permanent auction houses, from the flea head-quarters to the most elegant establishments, hold sales at regular, stated periods—semi-weekly, weekly, monthly, or whatever. Other dates are announced to sell out an estate, or when the independent auctioneer accumulates enough to warrant a day's auction.

Many city auction houses close for the summer (which brings the flowering of the galleries that operate in vacation areas during the summer only), but from September to June different days and hours are set for a particular kind of sale. Furniture, antiques and decorations might be auctioned on Friday and Saturday afternoons; important fine art on Wednesday evenings, specialties on other weekday afternoons.

Exhibitions

In 1682, the London Gazette advised auction-goers that the goods "will be exposed to sale . . . on

Thursday 12th, Friday 13th and Saturday 14th of
this instant March, at Mrs. Smythers Coffee House
on Thames Street, by the Custom House: The
said Paintings are to be viewed from this day
forward until all be sold. Catalogues may be had at
the place of sale." (Said catalogue requested
"Pray read me, but do not take me from the
Table.")

"It's our business to make everything look as good
as possible," one of the country's most important
auctioneers explained to me. "We try to point
out the defects, but we're not infallible, and this is
a grown up game. So come to the exhibition and
examine." Just as the auction is about to begin, he
announces to the audience, "If you haven't been
to the exhibition, please sit here and enjoy yourself,
but please don't buy anything you haven't seen
unless you know very well what you're doing."

"Then after all that," he tells me, "someone comes
up here and bids like mad on something they're
seeing for the first time; when they come to
collect it they say with dismay, 'I thought it was
pink and it's blue!'"

At important auctions exhibitions are never held on
the day of the sale, only before. Preview days are
announced in the ads. It's less fun, maybe, but go
to the exhibition and leave a bid if you want something and can't make the auction. The day of
the exhibition is the day people should decide what
they want to bid on.

At smaller auctions the preview might be held from,
say, 8 a.m. to 10 a.m., then a bell would ring
and everyone is shooed into their seats. "The
auction is about to start," the helpers call out.

"She was a very peculiar woman; she could hum as she talked, both at the same time. Weird. She was also a Kleptomaniac, which we knew. There were four of us watching her. She got interested in a very valuable glass creamer. How she did it I don't know, but she got away with it, and not one of us knew it until later."

The exhibition room doors (if any) are then closed off. No inspection is ever allowed after a sale starts.

At the exhibition, the merchandise on display can be handled (carefully). If the customer breaks something some auctioneers say they'll ask him to pay a reasonable amount for it; others just shrug and say "What can we do?" (Children aren't allowed in the exhibition hall.) There are all kinds of people at good auctions to help you examine things. They'll tip up furniture for you, take out drawers, open locked cases. Certain galleries will even lend you a black light to look at a painting with — it's like an x-ray and will show any over-painting and sometimes reveal a signature.

Most galleries have an elaborate alarm system and several employees on the premises, so they lose very little through theft. Some time ago a well-known gallery on Cape Cod presented a pre-sale exhibition to which a very rich woman came in a chauffeur driven car. "We knew her," the auctioneer says. "She was a very peculiar woman; she could hum as she talked, both at the same time. Weird. She was also a kleptomaniac, which we knew. There were four of us watching her. She got interested in a very valuable glass creamer. How she did it I don't know, but she got away with it, and not one of us knew it until later. I never got it back, either. I heard later that if I had sent her husband a bill he would have paid it."

Atmosphere

The surroundings at auctions are in keeping with the goods being sold. The two-bit kind are usually in dusty rented halls, the 'exhibition' a variety of

14

new and old junk and bargains spread out on tables. Folding chairs are shuffled around while people chatter and go back and forth.

The atmosphere of a blue-ribbon auction has been described as "something like that of a plush gambling casino: suave, chic, an exercise in mystery and intrigue in which elemental desires are scarcely concealed beneath starched shirt fronts and glittering gowns."

The middle ground is the efficient, plain, but comfortable auction gallery lined with displays or with adjoining exhibition halls that look like cluttered living rooms. The auctioneer may sit at a little side table with a microphone, or stand on a podium, while his helpers bring in item by item. They hold the objects up over a center table for the seated audience to look at as the auctioneer begins his patter. The atmosphere is decorous but friendly, and often there's a refreshment stand at the back (maybe tended by the auctioneer's wife). Sometimes a city auction closes up for lunch, but usually they work right through.

This is the way it works

Except at low-end haphazard affairs, everything is put up by number. If there are 350 items in the sale, #350 is in back, #1 in front. When a buyer enters the auction house he is given a card with his bidding number written large and black, perhaps with some conditions of sale printed on the back. His name and address are taken. When the auctioneer calls out, "Sold to Number 23," a clerk sits and writes a bill of sale for Number 23 and adds to it when Number 23 makes additional

15

purchases. She writes 60 to 80 an hour, as the auctioneer sells. At such sales people are assumed to have been to the exhibition and the auctioneer doesn't have to spend a lot of time describing everything.

At the famous galleries, each department has its own expert who usually acts as auctioneer for his specialty. Even in elegant city surroundings it's quite *de rigeur* to bring your lunch and munch away while keeping your eye out for the Great Buy that's coming up any minute. Everyone is thrown in together: rival dealers, collectors, neophytes, spectators—with one exception: during their jam-packed world famous special sales, Parke-Bernet has a "Gallery A" lesser region where the second-string buyers are relegated to watch the proceedings on closed-circuit TV. One time applause burst forth as a member of the "A" team successfully bid for a Renoir. The cheering brought a gale of laughter from the tonier main auction room, but the auctioneer was impressed; he said, "We'll certainly seat you down here next time, sir."

The auctionry bewares

1. Beware mistaken assumptions about the catalogues.

The small auction's "catalogue" may be only a mimeographed list of the pieces for sale. It should never be used as a guide to age or genuineness. Even if a real catalogue reads "attributed to" or "x type," that's no guarantee. The auctioneer is responsible only for what a catalogue says

16

definitely. If there is no catalogue you have no recourse, no matter what the auctioneer claims or implies—if it's not written down, you're out of luck.

2. Beware again and again, not to buy anything you haven't looked over first.

Even the most astute and experienced can get stung. A knowledgeable dealer told me he bid on a "Pennsylvania chalk" figure at a distance, without handling it personally, and paid $150. When he got it back to his shop he found it was of Mexican clay and he had to put it in his stock with a $15 price tag.

3. Beware, if you are spending real money, the fly-by-nights, the one day itinerant sale.

Find out who they are and where they come from. And if there's no chance to look things over first, don't go at all.

4. Beware the semi-auction, where dealers and others can buy things from the exhibition before the auction starts.

That's a most unethical practice, and can some-times be spotted. Suppose, for instance, an item has been advertised, and you've come to the sale especially for that reason, but you can't find it there anywhere. If you inquire about it the auctioneer will inevitably answer with "It got broken," or "stolen," or "lost." There are, on rare occasions, honest errors, but generally that kind of auction is better stayed away from. One auctioneer says, "I won't sell it to my best friend if it's been advertised." (He doesn't say what he'd do if it weren't mentioned in the ad.)

5. Beware until you know what kind of people you're doing business with.

Reputation is usually built on performance and gets around to the public mind. You can check with the Better Business Bureau, if you have doubts, or the trust department of a bank you do business with. "Ask around," says the auctioneer, "but remember, dealers frequently have a grudge against an auctioneer, so go to more than one person for advice." The expert consensus is to take the same precautions you would if you were going to deal with a builder or a lawyer.

6. Beware the out and out gyps.

Often referred to as "Atlantic City type auctions," these flim-flams also take place in Asbury Park, in Florida, in California — any place that's a winter resort area. "They're not selling the kind of things they advertise. These guys go to the New York gift shows and buy acres of stuff. They buy from jewelers on a wholesale basis, and they're using a so-called 'auction' to get retail and better prices," says a well-known auctioneer.

"It's pathetic. Hundreds of dollars spent by little working people, their savings, people who are getting taken. Those crooks claim they're estate sales but you can see the merchandise is mostly brand new, even if it looks beat up.

"First there's a five- to ten-minute description, during which members of the firm are out talking to the audience, asking where they're from, and so on. I saw a white-haired tourist type sitting there reading a newspaper. The auctioneer, who was finally auctioning instead of describing, says to the white-haired-man. 'You'll say 50?' He looks up

18

from his paper briefly, says 'uh-huh,'' and goes back to reading. The only thing that could have improved the blatancy was a sign hung on him reading 'shill.'"

7. Beware similar practices in the big city.

In cities like London and New York mock auctions are designed to pull in strangers off the street, using well-known brands of merchandise as bait for bilking them.

A favorite trick is to sell "surprise packages," (and boy, will you be surprised) which will be delivered later in the proceedings (to be opened when it's too late) and thereby keep the suckers hanging around—"jamming" they call it. Auctioneers who are masters at this game sell good quality items to stooges very cheap, setting up the suckers for the kill; then they replace the quality goods with junk. They are very adept at sleight of hand. You wouldn't think they could fool otherwise intelligent people but they are surprisingly skilled operators. These characters are always on the lookout for the police, of course, and their warning cry, equivalent to the Carnies' "Hey Rube," is "Bring out item number seven."

Some legitimate auctioneers say, "The auction business is beset with unsavory relatives, like the quack doctor or the ambulance-chasing lawyer. They should be put in jail. They're legalized con games." However, in the opinion of most auctioneers, these disgraces to the profession are dying out. "The auction business used to be free-for-alls, but in the last 100 years regulations have created first-class auction brokers. The auction business for the most part has become very respectable."

"I once bid a quarter on a huge moose head. All the time the auctioneer was looking for another bid, my wife was scanning the crowd for a good divorce lawyer."

2

BIDDING

"I once bid a quarter on a huge moose head. All the time the auctioneer was looking for another bid, my wife was scanning the crowd for a good divorce lawyer. She got even by buying a broken cement mixer so I could build a concrete driveway." — *Farmer's Magazine*

Two thousand years ago a Roman biographer wrote of an auction run by the Emperor Caligula to raise money on the palace furniture. "During the sale," Suetonius reported, "the Emperor noticed that Aponius had fallen asleep on his bench. Caligula told the auctioneer that every time the old man's head nodded, he was to take it as a bid." When the unfortunate Aponius finally woke up, he discovered he had purchased 347,000 talents worth of royal furniture — whether he liked it or not.

The moral of that story is don't go to auctions run by crooked emperors. But don't worry about scratching your nose, either. Those auctioneers are pretty smart fellows, and really don't conduct their business like the skit in which Dick Van Dyke raises his hand absent-mindedly while an awful picture is just being held up by the auctioneer — his for $50! His wife: "What did you do?" He: "I just raised my hand like this!" Auctioneer: "Yours for $100!"

Auctions, here we come

If you're off to your first auction, just decide you're going to be level-headed. At the same time keep in mind that you're new at all this. Your first auction will probably be an intoxicating experience, so the best place to keep your cool would be at an unimportant sale or country auction.

First, tattoo on the back of your bidding hand: CAVEAT EMPTOR (Let the buyer beware). Then, after you've looked everything over, write down what you're interested in and how much you're willing to pay for it. Every auctioneer will say it over and over: decide on the maximum you'll pay *before* the bidding starts, then WRITE IT DOWN.

When you're ready to get your feet wet, put one toe in by bidding small on a few things just to get the feel of it. But before you start, look and listen for a while. When an item you want comes up, listen to the first couple of bids. Don't get excited so everyone can see—that arouses competition. Be cool, don't bat an eye. Try to control your expression, even if it makes you feel like a secret agent. Just sound calm and raise your hand so the auctioneer can see it.

Some time or other you're bound to get bombed on the action—*everybody* goes nuts at auctions occasionally, even those hardened characters, the dealers. One of them told me he was bidding on a painting and, after allowing himself 10% leeway, arrived at his top figure. Suddenly he found himself bidding three times that amount before he could stop! He broke out in a cold sweat. But he was lucky; somebody else bid and he was off the hook.

22

The name for the disease that struck him is Auction Fever. It's the sheer inability to stop bidding. The former director of the Boston Museum told me, "Your palms begin to sweat, you can feel your face getting red, your heart begins to pound, and you cannot stop." It may sound like love, but it's auction fever.

Two hundred years ago, Dr. Johnson observed bidders at auctions: "The glitter in their eyes, the flush gaining their cheeks, the tremble of their uplifted heads, the expression of dismay or exulta- tion when the item is finally knocked down! As the sale progresses the room becomes surcharged with excitement, dramatic intensity is increasing because this excitement is partially suppressed. And now is the time to beware, to steel yourself against impulsion, for the tension is highly contagious and demands ACTION! . . . Auction fever is a disease in itself, and even the casual bystander can be swept off by this curious virus."

You can try to avoid auction fever by bringing along someone to restrain you—although you can always step on his foot to shut him up, or dis- courage his restraining hand by biting it (you are not liable for damages if the restrainer suddenly goes mad and begins to bid). Do beware the dread scourge, when your heart pounds away and you suddenly *have* to have it. Refuse to raise your top figure, *no matter what.*

How much should you bid?

First of all, make sure whether you're bidding on the entire lot or just one piece of it. Sometimes fine china plates, for instance, like Royal Doulton or

23

fancy service plates, are put up singly, so if you hear 2, 2.50, 3, it's each, not all. Other things do go in lots, with one bid taking a whole set. Sometimes there is bidding on one item in a group, and the rest at that price—it's done that way because (a) auctioneers find it easier to get $9 each for six chairs than $53, and (b) some people aren't so good at figuring.

In figuring out generally how much to bid, the question is not only how much a particular item is worth; it's just as important to ask yourself if you can afford what you're doing.

Centuries ago in ancient China, when a monk died his belongings were auctioned off to his fellows. When the bidding got too high, the monk who acted as auctioneer used to remind them, "Better be thoughtful. You may regret it later." Auctioneers don't do that now, so enthusiastic novices have to steel themselves to resist the temptation stirred by excitement. The voice of experience says, "You can always say to yourself, 'If I can get it for that amount, it's worth it to me and I'll take it.' Many times you'll see it pass you by beyond that amount, and many of those times you'll breathe a sigh of relief."

Impulse bidding is what you must not, under any circumstances, do. Take the pledge: No Impulse Bidding. Engrave it on your forehead: bid only after making pre-auction decisions. With those virtuous words still on my guilty lips, I have no doubt that you will end up at least once with something like the Victorian bedsteps for which I once insanely opened my mouth on impulse and which, when triumphantly acquired, proved to be crudely held

24

together with new nails that stuck out. My bed is hardly two feet off the floor, but I *had* to have those miserable bedsteps.

The bidding

There are generally two bidding styles an auctioneer uses. With one, he asks for some specific amount as a starting bid. If none is forthcoming, he lowers the amount until a starter comes up—but remember, in that case, he's not making an instant appraisal of the article, just trying to get started.

The other way is to let the crowd offer first. All such bids are gravely announced, although the other bidders rarely let a ridiculously low one stand.

The auctioneer doesn't mind a bit if you bid and don't buy. All bidders help him, even if they quit at low figures, and a good-natured stock joke is "That fellow bid 27 times, and hasn't bought a thing yet!"

The people who say they "missed all the good ones" are usually those who waited too long to bid. You have to speak up and not be shy. If the auctioneer can't see or hear your bid, you're going to lose something you want. And if you take too long to make up your mind, it's going to get knocked down while you're still deciding whether to open your mouth.

Things move fast, so anyone who wants to know what's going on has to pay attention. They really have to stay alert. I've seen people raise their own bid, from enthusiasm and inattention. And as the habitué says, "Know at all times where your mate is standing during the sale. Otherwise you might discover that the stubborn beast who keeps bidding you up is your wife."

Friends and rivals

It sometimes happens that you and a friend at the auction want the same thing, in which case it's fair to agree that the first one who expressed an interest gets to try for it. It also happens occasionally that pals have both been seized with a blind passion for the same object and have fallen to wildly bidding each other up.

At an auction in Boston once, two rich dowagers from distinguished families both wanted an ordinary doctor's scale which was hard to find at the time. Each was determined to have it. The auction gallery where the battle took place says that as the bidding mounted, steel and vitriol were in the air. "The action became hysterical and so did the audience. That scale went for a ridiculously high sum and the loser never spoke to the winner again." Surely it's unusual for people to get so emotional just over an auction? One auctioneer puts it this way: "I've seen guys ready to fight—big ones, too. When people are determined to get something, they're nuts. I've seen them stick their hand up and keep it there. Every time I called for a new bid, that hand was still up, so determined to get it!"

But that won't happen to you if you remember this: There Will Be Other Sales. Don't be carried away by fervor.

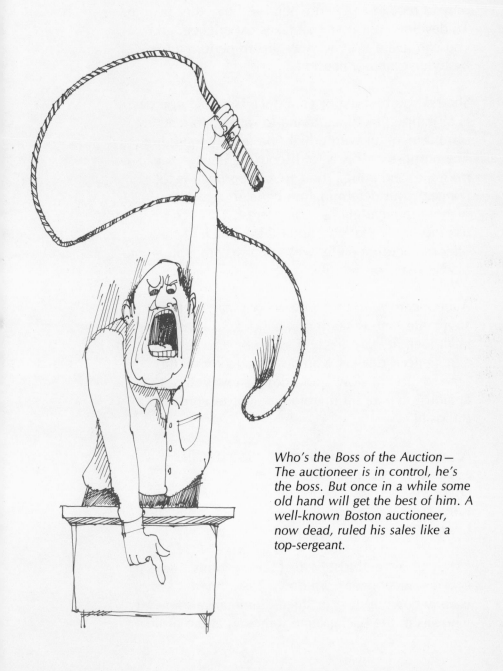

*Who's the Boss of the Auction —
The auctioneer is in control, he's
the boss. But once in a while some
old hand will get the best of him. A
well-known Boston auctioneer,
now dead, ruled his sales like a
top-sergeant.*

Strategy

Strategy is the name of the bidding game. For the novice, it's helpful to know the basic strategies, if only to recognize them when used by other people. To develop your own just takes experience, and you can live a Walter Mitty dream performance by trying different methods.

Should you be bold or cautious? The bold approach is to jump in feet first, trying to rout opponents by starting right off with a high, preferably loud, bid. The purpose of this is to discourage competitors from the beginning. The careful approach is to conceal your determination beneath a tentative manner, pretending lack of interest. This can be used to imply that you don't think much of the offering, and hopefully will lull any competitors into a false sense of security.

Auctioneers warn that wily waiting can be tricky. Very little time is spent on each lot, so if you hold back long, it's not likely you're going to get it. But experienced dealers who buy at auction all the time say to bid slowly and don't show you're too anxious, to wait till the bidding almost comes to a standstill.

As for opening the bidding, a Chicago gallery advises, "Never open the bidding right away. Only come in when the auctioneer slows down. Don't forget, the auctioneer never says 'Sold' while the bidding is fast."

"There'll be ten bids the first few seconds," says a country auctioneer from down East, "then it's usually down to two or three. Sometimes some guy who sits in the background jumps in at the limit, just as I'm about to bang down Sold. I always announce it when there's a new bidder.''

Even experienced auction-goers have been bluffed out of the bidding. It might happen because two other bidders are locked in a contest of wills; or some nut with all kinds of money will throw in ridiculous bids; or some dealer will try to maneuver you out of jumping the increment by $30, for example, instead of $10. But you too can work that ploy.

Increments

Increments are the amount the bid increases by. The auctioneer usually indicates the increment he'd prefer by saying something like "I have 25, who will say 50?" You don't have to follow his lead; the increment depends on the value of the object. Often he will decrease the suggested jump when hot bidding cools down. "You have to watch the tens," says a British expert, "because most people think in decimals."

Here's a description of an estate auction when they put up a blue Staffordshire American-scene platter of the kind the British made for the American trade after the Revolutionary War:

"The auctioneer calls for a bid of $50, it goes on to $100, $150, $200, on up to $350. Now the audience begins to sit up and take notice. $400, $450, $500 — it's slowing down. Suddenly it begins to gain: $600, $700, $800, electrifying the audience. Not many of them know the difference between Staffordshire paste and anchovy paste, but they crane their necks and their hearts get to thumping. One of the remaining contenders bids $950 and it hangs there, the audience holding its breath. Then the other shakes his head and the auctioneer's gravel comes down with a bang and the whole crowd bursts into applause, as though for a star in the theater."

An important dealer in the Merchandise Mart told me he doesn't jump at the units already set—he breaks the rhythm. "That makes me known as a salesroom pest, but I get what I want." An auctioneer he has probably done it to claims "One cheap bid invites another. If you really want to knock someone off, double the bid; or if it's going up at, say, $5 intervals, jump it to $10 intervals."

"However," says the calm owner of the most prestigious auction house in the mid-West, "in a competitive environment, why blow your wad all at one time? It's the essence of auction sales to buy as cheaply as possible."

Another dealer's trick of the trade is to open the bid at about half of what he's willing to pay, then jump it to near his limit. "This," he says, often discourages competition by suggesting the sale is rigged."

Usually if you've outbid the dealer, you've won. Whatever the dealer pays for something, he has to get at least twice that price when he sells it, so you're buying it at the auction at wholesale or below. Our cynical observer says, "The dealer doesn't want people to see him bid, doesn't want them to know what he's buying. But if he's spending $50 it's worth $100 to me."

There are always exceptions, of course. A dealer

might be tilting with a rival, or bidding on commission for some customer. If you're following the
bidding of someone you recognize as your friendly
neighborhood dealer, you're picking his brains, and
if you do it too often, he can drop a bomb on
you — such as running something up to more than
it's worth.

I've seen dealers open almost every bid with $1, or
$3, or $5 on *anything,* never seeming to care what
it was. An auctioneer explained that strange
behavior to me later. "If he gets it for that, okay,
if not, he doesn't care; he just doesn't bid on it
again."

Non-professional buyers bid on things for
different reasons — sentimental reasons, like a piece
of furniture reminding them of one in their child-
hood, or on something special for a birthday
present. Items are sometimes bid up to what
they're worth to the bidder, but they're not worth
anywhere near that to you.

Who's the boss of the auction

When arguments develop over who bid what, in the
South they say, "Any trouble usually comes from
people who don't want anyone to see them bid
and sometimes the auctioneer can't see them
either."

The auctioneer is in control, he's the boss. But once
in a while some old hand will get the best of
him. A well-known Boston auctioneer, now dead,
ruled his sales like a top-sergeant. He once put up
four paintings of the Four Seasons and found that
a timid but determined neophyte wanted two of

them, while a former mayor (who had also been a governor) wanted the other two. The auctioneer refused to break up the set.

The mayor and the young man kept bidding each other up and up and up, until at last the mayor couldn't stand it any longer. He jumped up and yelled, "You damn fool! Why don't you shut up and let me buy the set and I'll sell you your two."

"Governor," said the auctioneer, "I didn't tell you how to run the state, don't you tell me how to run my business." But it was too late. The novice shut up. The mayor bought the set and promptly split it with him.

When the auctioneer decides to knock the goods down, he may do it suddenly; a sharp rap of the gavel means it's all over. Or he may warn the bidders with "Any further advance?," or "Fair warning," or "Going once," etc. "It's my option," a Los Angeles auctioneer says, "if the hammer comes down. If someone disputes the winning bidder and there's too much flak, I take it out of competition and save it for another time. That's my right by law."

There was a cliffhanger at Parke-Bernet when a 34-karat emerald ring was put up for sale and a wild contest gathered steam. Tension mounted as a rich New York matron bid by telephone against an Italian at the auction who was said to be bidding for Sophia Loren. A noisy argument broke out on the floor when, pushed to his limit, the Italian protested the bidding by telephone as completely unfair. But the auctioneer had the right to decide, and the telephone bidder ended up with the ring—for more than a quarter of a million dollars.

What happens if you overbid?

Don't overbid, ever. Even if you get the item, you won't enjoy it. Stop bidding when the object is no longer worth that price to you, and don't think in terms of just $5 more or $10 more; think of *total price*, which I trust you have written down in advance. Overbidding has been described as producing a pleasurable flush during, but afterwards it's akin to making love and getting the girl pregnant.

"It's tough for us," says the gallery owner, "when overbidders cry. We're operating with someone else's merchandise, which causes considerable problems if we have to cancel the sale." Another says, "Women have come up to me when the auction's over with tears in their eyes—their husbands will divorce them, or kill them they say—but nothing is supposed to be returnable. We're supposed to leave the buy as is unless it's been misrepresented. Listen, in traveling sales it's yours the minute you buy it, even if you throw fourteen kinds of fits."

Bidding signals

Some auction-goers use special codes so other people won't know what they're doing. Dealers want to hide their bids from rival dealers and private collectors. Collectors want to keep their business to themselves. Everyone wants to pretend he has no interest in a find so he won't lose his advantage. Then there's the fellow who whispered to the auctioneer, "I don't want my brother to know I'm bidding against him, so if I touch my pocket handkerchief . . ."

The Silent Gang — One of the scourges of auctioneers is the illegitimate buying ring, a group of people (almost always dealers) who agree among themselves not to compete with each other for something they all want.

Most signals are common procedure: the lift of a forefinger, the raised hand, a sound like "glup," a nod, or a certain number of fingers to indicate amount. Sometimes it's just meeting the auctioneers eye, or winking.

Private signals are arranged in advance with the auctioneer. A regular may say that if he keeps his cigar in his mouth it means he's bidding. Cigar out of mouth means he's done. Cigar in left hand means full raise of bid asked; in right hand means one-half raise.

Bidders may also have codes to signal partners (someone bidding for him to keep his identity secret): hat on says "bid"; hat off says "stop."

The most famous bidding confusion in memory resulted from the sale of Rembrandt's "Titus" at Christie's in London. A pre-auction agreement in writing stipulated that when Mr. Norton Simon, the well-known industrialist and art connoisseur, was sitting down, he was bidding. If he bid openly, he was also bidding. When he stood up, he had stopped bidding. If he sat down again, he was not bidding unless he raised his finger. Having raised his finger, he was bidding, until he stood up again. Not unreasonably, the auctioneer got confused. The painting was knocked down to another bidder, until Mr. Simon proved he had made the winning bid.

Even if we don't know all the time what's going on, the auctioneer has to announce the amount of the bid no matter what signals have been used. Don't be intimidated by the subtleties of tugs or twitches or removing the left shoe. Just watch the other

amateurs and do what they do. It's better not
to wave things around indiscriminately, though — it
can imperil your relations with the auctioneer.

The "Unreserved Auction"

An unreserved auction means that the highest
bidder takes the goods, no matter how low his bid.
That's the best kind of auction to go to.

Reams have been written about the question of
reserves, and it's still an argument between buyer
and seller that will probably never be settled. The
seller says he has to protect himself from ruin
by setting a minimum amount he will accept,
particularly in defense against buying rings
(which will be explained shortly). The buyer says
reserve prices are a hindrance to free bidding
and dampen the unsophisticated auction-goer's
eternal quest for bargains.

Some auctioneers won't accept merchandise with a
reserve price. Some just want to accept 'stop loss'
reserves — i.e. not take too big a loss. Every buyer
says that for the fairest auction look for the words
UNRESTRICTED or WITHOUT LIMIT OR RESERVE.
It's not of great concern to most of us, though,
because reserve prices are usually restricted only to
very important, expensive items.

When the auctioneer 'passes' something

Let's say some totally unreserved item should bring
at least $300. Someone calls out $25. The auctioneer
says "$25, give me $100;" he repeats it. No one
does. He passes it, since he can't let it go for so

36

much under value. He gives it back to the owner or he'll put it up some other time. "I'm not going to throw it away," he says. "No reserve is even implied; I'm just not going to throw it away." The rules are his to make, although auctioneers of lesser goods say this kind of thing makes disgruntled customers.

When you can't be there

The book-bid or order-bid is for bidding in absentia. Many exhibitions are held on days preceding the auction, and if you can only go there once, it's by far better to attend to the exhibition and leave an order bid. It's also common practice, especially with collectors, to bid from catalogues by mail, if they live too far away from a sale. The catalogue always says "If you are unable to attend the sale in person, we will bid for you."

A book-bid indicates the *maximum* amount you're willing to pay, but not by any means the amount you're going to have to pay. An employee of the house (who may be introduced as "not the richest woman in the world, just the bidder for order bids") bids for you just as if you were competing in person.

A buy-in is different, although it is also an absentee bid. If the bidding doesn't reach the reserve price, the auctioneer (or someone acting secretly for the consignor) then buys in (buys back) the object. The auctioneer has allowed the owner to leave an absentee bid at a price below which he will not sell his effects, and the auctioneer charges him about $1/3$ the standard commission that he would get if the piece had actually changed hands.

The silent gang

One of the scourges of auctioneers is the illegitimate buying ring, a group of people (almost always
dealers) who agree among themselves not to
compete with each other for something they all
want. One of them bids for all, thereby keeping
the price uncompetitively low. Then these knaves
have a private auction of their own, divvying up
the booty, while the original owner is out in the
cold with a big loss. It's a gyp and it's not legal, but
it's impossible, as they say in enforcement circles,
to apprehend the perpetrators.

Ring machinations have as many twists as a
Borgia plot (there are even rings within rings). After
they've gotten the item cheaply by reducing the
competition, they have a surreptitious "knock-out"
auction, where each member of the ring writes his
bid down secretly, highest taking the prize. Then
they split the profit, pro-rating it according to the
amount each bid. Everyone in on the clandestine
operation makes something on the deal, even the
little clod who actually doesn't have the cash or
inclination to bid at the auction anyway. At the
turn of the century, insiders were writing about
auction rings where they "knew some dealers in
the ring to attend sales for months, making a nice
weekly income of their divvy, though never bidding
or buying so much as a bed slat."

Rings (or buying slugs or kippers) are not always
subtle. Members have been seen blatantly signaling
each other. The smallest ring I ever heard of was
the fellow who said, "I gave the interior decorator
three pounds not to bid against me."

Ironically, rings do auction-goers a good turn by

38

keeping the price down. There have been sales where bidding was so light and prices so low that the outcome was shocking (and the denial of the presence of a ring absurd) — the consignor suffered tremendous losses and any knowledgeable buyer there could have done marvelously well for himself.

Normally rings operate only on very desirable objects, high-priced enough to make collusion worth their while. One auctioneer told me, "Important auctions always bring rings of unsavory dealers, and rings form only for silver, paintings, furniture, and decorations. I've never known a ring to form for anything else."

In 1776, while Americans were occupied with other matters, the French published a booklet titled *Confession Publique,* in which a famous French dealer told all. Among his sins he related how he and his companions rigged prices by getting together before an auction and agreeing to run up the bidding on things they wanted to unload. On the other side of the fence, if they spotted something good at the preview, two of them would stand near it and exclaim loudly, "Too bad it's only a copy." Since they were known experts, the remark usually worked. One of them would get the object for a fraction of its real value, the author confessed, and after he re-sold it, they would all divide their ill-gotten gains. Things haven't changed much since then.

The bidding bewares

1. Beware the bidding that is being "run" or "trotted."

That's when the auctioneer runs up the price by recognizing phantom bids. Maybe it's not just small-time cheats who do it—maybe the audience is shy to start; maybe the auctioneer manufactures a bid because he can't let an expensive thing go for nothing; maybe it's a defensive tactic against a ring. Whatever the reason, it's a deception. ("One-legged trotting" is when the auctioneer has only one bidder and pretends another; when he has no bidders, it's "two-legged.")

2. Beware asking who's bidding against you, if you suspect phantom bids.

Auctioneers have dozens of ways to avoid answering, so just drop out of the contest. If your suspicions are correct, don't be surprised if someone approaches you afterwards and explains that for some reason he doesn't need the item after all, and would you, as the next-highest bidder, like to take it off his hands for the amount of your last bid.

3. Beware the dealer who bids on his own merchandise.

An ethical auctioneer catching some dealer bidding on his own goods (obviously to run up the price), sends some one over to warn him. If he persists, the auctioneer will withdraw the merchandise from the auction. "Be leery of some guy who's opening 50% of the bids," one auctioneer says. "Even if the dealer asks to bid on his own stuff and pay his own commission, that's still shilling and it smells bad."

4. Beware the shill.

He's the fellow hired by the auctioneer (or the

seller) to make phony bids raising the price. Also called puffing or by-bidding, it's forbidden by law.

"Some auction galleries," says an old hand, "like Grant's, on Wabash Avenue in Chicago for 30 or 40 years—it's gone now—had three or four shills in the audience. Everyone knew it, but it was the only game in town."

5. Beware the friendly advice of a stranger.

Especially the one who tells you why what you are interested in isn't any good. And likewise the auction sharp, the badmouther who runs down a piece by mumbling criticisms as he looks it over. "He'll run a piece of furniture into the ground," says a young auctioneer who's just starting out, "and then buy it for $1000. If you're a novice and listen to them you'll never bid."

6. Beware the tout.

A kissing-cousin of the by-bidder (puffer, capper) he's a confederate of the auctioneer or owner, and he floats around the exhibition dropping a well-aimed word or two, "Look, there's a genuine Imari!" During the auction he stimulates bidding by audible remarks that are injections of adrenalin to flagging enthusiasm.

7. Beware to double-check the reputation of the auctioneer with whom you leave an order-bid.

Some not-so-upright type might use your limit as a lever to get higher bids—and then you're out the window.

But it's not all one-sided.

The auctioneer has to:

1. Beware the excuses launched at him by bidders trying to refuse to take what they bought.

These excuses can wax fanciful in the extreme, but the more pedestrian ones are: It isn't what I thought it was. My husband will kill me. I didn't know what I was doing. The law says the sale is as binding as a signed contract, but very often the auctioneer will put the item up again. If it happens more than once a cash deposit probably would be required before the offender is allowed to bid. An old New England auctioneer tells about the time someone refused an item he had been high bidder on. The auctioneer "tried nicely to force him to take it, but no go." So he put it up again, and the refuser had the nerve to enter the bidding! The auctioneer says he knocked it down fast to another bidder.

2. Beware the bidder who can single-handedly depress auction prices.

This clever fellow interrupts the rhythm of the auction with some attention-getting distraction. It's like the maneuver in football when the defense tries to slow down the opposition by calling time out, interrupting a successful offensive drive.

An auctioneer tells, for instance, how one fellow called out an impertinent question as the price of some real estate was rising fast. He succeeded in his design to interrupt the flow of bidding and profited mightily by his ploy. That sort of thing is actually unlawful, and sellers have been known to sue when large amounts of money were involved.

42

3. Beware the dealer who not only depresses prices by making disparaging remarks about an object at the exhibition, but has been known to propose a joint buying arrangement with an interested bidder "to prevent the bidding up of the price." (Then this villain reneges on the agreement after the sucker has acquired the item).

4. Beware the private buyer who gets something at an outrageously low price by sending a proxy bidder who sniffs and sniffles and enlists everyone's sympathy, such as the widow or raggedly dressed daughter at an estate sale. Who wouldn't be reluctant to bid against them?

The auction is a floating crap game, all right. But it's admittedly the most exhilarating form yet invented for changing ownership of merchandise. "It's a form of entertainment," say the followers of the game, "like the theater or a horserace. Besides, you always come home with something instead of just a torn ticket."

"It's like hero worship of a horsetrainer — women become fascinated with auctioneers. Auctioneers have to have personal magnetism. . . .

3

THE AUCTIONEER

"Each of the three women I've married I've met through the auction business. They were all customers.

"If the auctioneer is half-way decent looking with a little personality and a little sex appeal . . . A leading authoress—this gal calls me up, 'Oh, I want you to come over and look at this new flaubrit and give me an appraisal.' If I had a dollar for every time one of these women answers the door in a negligee!

"It's like hero worship of a horsetrainer—women become fascinated with auctioneers. Auctioneers have to have personal magnetism, they have to have personality—because they're salesmen."— verbatim transcript of my interview with a veteran big city auctioneer.

The auctioneer's job

For an auction to be a good one, the first requirement is a good auctioneer in charge of the show. If he's good, he has the situation well in hand. He recognizes what he's selling, presents it properly, and carefully points out defects without hullabaloo.

He keeps going at a good clip, not so fast as to lose bids, but without dragging it out for a few more dollars. "If the bidding is ended," says one, "sell the item. If I start trying to pull out another bid, people will expect it every time and hold back their bids. But if they know they've got to bid in a hurry, they'll keep on their toes."

Another auctioneer says the skillful practitioner watches his audience as an actor does. Eventually interest will start to flag. To wake everyone up he takes a good article of value and knocks it down fast to the first bidder (who, hopefully, is you). Everybody perks up, he says, and waits for lightning to strike twice. A rural auctioneer talks about working on the audience to get them to bid more, but if you look poor and hesitant he "won't work on you too hard for money."

Auctioneers have a great deal of freedom in organizing the sale and setting up the conditions of the auction. They have a variety of legal responsibilities and protection—between the auctioneer and the seller and between the auctioneer and the buyer (one of his powers is the prerogative to refuse bids from minors, insolvents, drunks, and the mentally irresponsible). His ultimate goal is to increase prices by arousing competition among the bidders, and it's nerve-racking work.

What manner of man is this

You won't be long at the auction before you say to yourself, like every auction buff before you, "What a ham!" Some auctioneers are smoother than others, but they're all actors. And they have to play varying roles without the lines a playwright provides an actor. The auctioneer has to compose his own as he goes along, creating his role to sell to different buyers, remembering at the same time that he has to be careful not to offend people and ruin a sale.

In addition to being a performer, he's part businessman and part psychologist. He has to keep his sense of perspective, his eyesight has to be good, his judgments fast and accurate. One describes the auctioneer's professional persona this way: "He has to keep everyone in good humor, and cope with wiseacres and hecklers and petty spoilers (who have it in for some dealer there, or are trying to get even with a former customer). Sometimes a man of so many parts lets his power go to his head—or maybe that's why he becomes an auctioneer in the first place—he's in the perfect eye of power."

A dynamic, independent city auctioneer puts his ego right on the line: "Remember, the auctioneer is God up there. Collectors need us. They cater to us. I could go out to dinner every night if I wanted to. 'Call me first,' they tell me, 'when you have something good.' Everybody wants to be on your good side—sports figures, politicians, everyone who collects." Although it's difficult to find gifts for an auctioneer, this one was an amateur horseman, and one collector sent him a saddle in appreciation for a painting he had tipped him off to and for which the collector had bid successfully. The auctioneer told me he was bragging about the gift when he read that "a certain prominent American" had bought the painting from the bidder for ten times what he paid at the auction for it. "He should have sent me the horse, too," the auctioneer added.

In 1916 a collector wrote, "The auction theory I have is never to offend the auctioneer. He's a sensitive soul full of pride in his profession, and if you irritate him by some subtle pyschological process, he will make the crowd go on bidding. I don't know quite how he does it, I am merely aware that he can. Because of my flattering deference an excellent bargain was dropped into my waiting hands."

Most of today's auctioneers say their obligation is to their consignor to get the best price possible, whether they like the bidder or not. "We work for the consignor and we don't care who buys." They also claim that, "Buyers at auction in pick-up trucks or Cadillacs all look alike and are treated alike."

The auctioneer's technique

It may seem as though the auctioneer is up there merely recognizing bidders in turn and announcing their bids. What he's really doing is promoting the interest of potential buyers and enlivening the bidding. You won't remember that part of it when you've left the auction, but he's been maintaining audience interest right along with remarks like, "Ladies and gentlemen, this is the best example of Victorian silver I've ever seen," or "This French Provincial table is worth a lot more than that," or "A much more ordinary Sandwich plate went for twice that price last week," or "I think I have a real sleeper here." ("That," says the professional, "means it's going cheaply. Everything is a sleeper if you buy it cheaply enough.")

"A little joke doesn't hurt," auctioneers say (as long

48

as it doesn't delay the proceedings), "and talking nice to the ladies can work wonders." Bits of humor are used to loosen up the tense spectators and then keep the bidding ball rolling, filling in a lull or a delay. It's not good for business if the auctioneer becomes a comic in the eyes of prospective buyers, but they're a glib lot, and they need to be.

A Cape Cod auctioneer tells how early in his career he made the mistake of having the merchandise between him and the audience, where he couldn't see it all. He was extolling the virtues of a chest of drawers when the audience started laughing. The more he talked, the more they laughed. Finally he got off the block and came out to look. One support had broken and the drawers on that side were sagging drunkenly toward the floor. "Well," he said, pulling the audience right back to him, "when you're as old as that piece, your drawers will be sagging too."

The urban (and urbane) auctioneer never embarrasses anyone. If loud voices and audible comments are disrupting the tenor of the sale, the auctioneer has to take interest away from the disturbance. If that doesn't shut them up, he will probably ask the talkers to please carry on their conversation elsewhere. The hick auctioneer can be cruder. One oldtimer only likes to sell where he's known "or else there's nobody to joke with, nobody to call by name, and nobody to pick on."

The performance of the auctioneer depends considerably on the kind of audience he's facing, but he creates an atmosphere too. His sales promotion efforts can create noise and confusion, a kind of carnival air. Auctions in cities are usually quite sedate, but at even the most dignified of them

the auctioneer creates a climate of tension that
arcs in crescendos and diminuendos till the
sudden end.

The chant

That singsong rolling forward is a rhythmic,
spine-tingling chant intended to seduce. Sometimes
it's staccato and incomprehensible, sounds pouring
out like gravel down a chute, needing a decoding
expert until the word SOLD reassures us it's
English. Usually there's no difficulty at all under-
standing the exciting rush: 5 bid, do I hear 6, 6, 7,
6, I hear 6, 7, 6 all done, are you through? Or,
22½, now 5, 25 bid, 7½, 25 27½, 25, all through
at 25? are you all done?

Styles vary with the auction and you'll hear "Gimme
20, gimme 20, do I hear 20? SOLD for 15!" as
well as "and NOW make it 350, do I have 50
thank you sir the bid is 50 NOW make it 75 who
will make it 75 NOW make it 75 who will make
it 75 NOW make it 400 who will give me 25
25 25?

If the bidding is very brisk you probably won't get
the benefit of the songs, just a call of the raises.
Chanting, like patter, is the auctioneer's way to
entertain while he promotes sales. It makes intervals
between bids less obvious and obscures the fact
that the bidding may be anything but lively. The
auctioneer considers chanting a voice-saver too, for
as in singing, it comes from the diaphragm and
eases the strain on the vocal chords.

If you aren't interested in a particular lot being
sold and watch the chant instead, you'll notice the
auctioneer doesn't repeat the same words or phrases.

50

In a few minutes he had bought a boat for which he had very little use, since he lived several hundred miles from any body of water larger than a bathtub.

The better he is the more he varies them.
"Want to make it six? Now six? Who will give me six? I have six. Will you give me seven. Do I hear seven? Will you take it at seven?"

The pace

A skillful auctioneer keeps bidders on their toes. He might set a fast pace by starting with some particularly interesting items and knocking them down quickly. At certain auctions, if the audience is losing interest, the auctioneer might quicken the pace again by switching to a different line of goods to stimulate different bidders. One successful auctioneer even drops a breakable item occasionally in order to wake up the audience and at the same time to put them in a jolly mood.

Auctioneers use what they call "a quick hammer" to encourage bidders to respond quickly. They know they may sometimes miss a bid by running the auction through fast, but they expect to make up for it on other items. On the other hand, a chief auctioneer at Parke-Bernet says he can't simply say "I have $5000, any more?" and then bang down the hammer, because the consignor would feel that there were bids 'left in the room.'"

"It's easy," says another, "to get it over with and bring the gavel down SOLD. It's the waiting that calls for great auctioneering (and if you're the bidder, you know what that wait means, waiting to see if someone tops your bid)."

The stories are legion of skillful auctioneers from whom experienced people buy crazy things they have no use in this world for. One is told by a super-salesman who was on his way to close a deal when he saw a crowd gathered on a nearby lawn. Since he was still early for his appointment, he moseyed over to listen for a few minutes. So sweet was the auctioneer's siren song that it was impossible to resist. In a few minutes he had bought a boat for which he had very little use, since he lived several hundred miles from any body of water larger than a bathtub.

Even those in the profession are not immune. The widow of a leading auctioneer tells how he found himself one day at a country auction (home of most of these legends) where the rural auctioneer was having a hard time. The city auctioneer felt sorry for him and to help him out threw in a couple of bids. He ended up with a cow, "And before he could get rid of it, the cow had calves that he had to put up with too!" she says.

The Colonel and the Lieutenant

A great many hinterland auctioneers sign themselves "Colonel," (some gracefully putting quotation marks around it), a right an auctioneer acquires by working his way through an undisclosed amount of used articles. Auction schools also confer the title on their graduates. These colonels are about as military as the head of Kentucky Fried Chicken, but the title is thought to have originated when real Army Colonels after the Civil War were ordered to sell surplus property to the highest bidder. ("When we go to meetings," says a small-towner, "everybody calls everybody else colonel.")

The auctioneer's lieutenants are "feeders" and "runners." Runners do just that—they fetch and carry. A feeder, or floorman, often acts as manager while the auction goes on. He hands items up to the auctioneer, and helps him with a quick description if necessary. At less tightly organized sales he feeds items at the right time for the best prices, all the while gauging the crowd for what they want put up, and he points out bidders to the auctioneer and buyers to the runners. A certain village auctioneer says that when he's hung up on the first bid, his feeder keeps adding items until a second bid is received. "It's done so casually," he says, "the crowd will never know." (But now you do).

Auction Pete says there's also a cleanup man — "Whatever is left is his; like if something wasn't sold, or if you forgot to pick something up."

Most licensed auctioneers are appraisers, too, a part of the profession that has added attractions for its members who are swingers. "I've made love to more women doing appraisal work and auctioning —I could write a book," one good-looking auctioneer with a lot of nervous vitality says. "It's a perfect out for a married woman — the auctioneer can be seen with her during the day with a legitimate excuse. He is respected in the community, easy to be with; no one can complain if he's seeing a woman in the afternoon, giving her advice on her collection."

The Auctioneer Bewares

1. Beware the "country boy approach" some rural auctioneers boast about, deemed "endearing to friends and strangers alike" by a colleague who should know better.

Such a suspenders-snapper likes to make "embarrassing wisecracks, making someone in the audience the butt," no doubt for the amusement of the rubes. They could promise me a 1710 butterfly table for $5 and I wouldn't be within 20 miles of his place. It's hard to believe there would be auction-goers so naïve, but said colleague claims some fall for a Yankee-type auctioneer" who often sells barefoot, disarming everyone."

2. Beware any auctioneer who can't produce the item you successfully bid on.

"It broke before you came for it," they might say, or "I'm so sorry, we can't find it, it's missing!" or someone took it, or he wasn't supposed to sell it, it was a mistake. You say you bid and got it, he says he can't find it—what can you do, sue him? Some things can be stolen or delivered to the wrong person or broken. But it's extremely rare. Just watch if it happens more than once.

3. Beware what you *think* the auctioneer is saying.

Certain types to be wary of make general statements that really mean nothing, but can give the wrong impression by using key words that mean a lot. Some, it is reported, like to talk like this: "That pitcher looks a lot like GENUINE CUT GLASS;" or "I wouldn't be surprised if THIS IS A VALUABLE ANTIQUE."

4. Beware what certain auctioneers call "various selling techniques," better defined as the old shell game.

One old rogue says he pulled such a "technique" on a "heckler" who opened the bidding at one dollar on every item put up, regardless of it's worth. "This old routine we dig out from time to time," he says, "comes after selling something for very little despite pleading for larger bids." The so-called heckler muttered "junk," at which Mr. Sharp Auctioneer tipped it over and a $5 bill fell out. He says, "My feeder slipped it in at the right time." (These guys are never seen by the audience — they're as slick as a graduate pickpocket). Prices picked up and they undoubtedly got their $5 back several times.

5. Beware the sort of another sharp practice this same hick auctioneer is amused by, a legslapper he calls a "real old chestnut."

He puts a box up, and tells the crowd the truth about it — that its contents cost $125, are still brand new, have never been used and are in perfect condition. "A wiseguy," he writes, "who had been trying to cut bids down for the first hour paid $9 for it, as I sold it to him the moment he jumped into the bidding. He was rewarded with a set of false teeth and the laughter of the crowd."

6. Beware the out-and-out crook, the rural auctioneer, who makes fun of each thing a certain person buys.

He intimates every item this particular bidder calls out on is junk, until the crowd laughs each time he bids. What a haul these two make, splitting the profits at the end on some fine piece they got for next to nothing.

Auctioneers come in all sizes and shapes and personalities. I've talked to soft-spoken mild ones, to dynamic nervous ones, to easy-going charmers,

to correct up-tight ones, to ungrammatical hicks.
They come in packages ranging from swinging mod
to wispy grandfatherly, and occasionally in print
dresses and Dr. Locke shoes. Their forebears are
equally varied, from red-haired Celtic to black-eyed
Middle-Eastern, and all the countries in between.
They're all American businessmen, and most of
them are successful and astute. It's a good idea to
remember that, when you think you've got one who
doesn't know what he's selling.

*That singsong forward is a
rhythmic, spine-tingling chant
intended to seduce.*

The "mystery package," with its allure of untold riches, is one of the favorite hunting grounds for finds.

4

WHAT TO BUY—In General

"Do not ever believe friends who say, 'Why didn't you buy that pot-bellied stove for me?' You will discover that your friends don't really want all those things they appear to crave when you are showing them your junk collection. Let them buy their own pot-bellied stoves." — The Farmers' Magazine

Goods put on the auction block encompass everything imaginable, up to and including an empire. In the year 193, the whole Roman Empire was auctioned off by the Praetorian Guard. Didius Julianus, who outbid everyone else for the defunct Emperor's crown, didn't get a very good buy, though; he only wore the crown for two months before the next usurper cut his head off under it.

The offerings at auctions fall into three categories: what you could kick yourself for not buying; what you were astute enough to resist; and what you bought and now look at with pleasure and satisfaction.

Despite the endless variety, furnishings and the decorative arts remain the staple merchandise of auctions. The most interesting objects are those crafted with hand tools, and the best of them excel in taste, materials and workmanship. There is, of course, a limited supply of excellent handcrafted merchandise available, since the complex economics of mass production have virtually eliminated the individual craftsman of a by-gone time.

The nostalgia factor

This seems to be the era of the great nostalgia kick, not the least of whose proponents are the younger generation. Price records are being set all over at auctions like those that sell thousands of articles from the 1920s to the 1940s. Objects from an earlier age are even more popular: an old kerosene peanut roasting machine from the 1890s was crated for immediate shipment as soon as it was bought at a recent auction in Pennsylvania, and was sold upon arrival in South Carolina for triple what it cost the successful bidder. One fellow flew in from California just for that Pennsylvania sale and purchased, among other things, a twelve-foot long United Cigar Store sign, for which he was offered a $50 profit within ten minutes. Why all this fuss over such things? The answer is nostalgia, and perhaps growing awareness of our past.

Why would anyone pay good money for an old bottle? Well, it could have historical or educational value. For instance, a bottle made in the shape of a log cabin at the time of Benjamin Harrison's presidential campaign had the maker's name impressed on it, E. G. Booz, and admirers of Harrison were partial to the whiskey in it.

People who pay a lot for a copy of the Constitution are really buying an ingredient of romance. It's what the document says that is of vital interest, and you can read its text in a number of books. Still, it's like the attraction of a recent auction in New Jersey selling the contents of the Old Brick Church, stained glass and pews included. Or the Gay 90s Museum in Quincy, Illinois, which auctioned off everything from nickelodeons and sleighs to a Harley Davidson motorcycle. Or the Pittsburgh Landmarks Foundation, which rescues things from buildings slated for demolition—like the last of certain commercial lampshades and a leaded glass window with alchemical symbols—and puts them up for auction to support the Foundation. Some of nostalgic merchandise may be campy, but many are items from the past which are durable, often grotesque, and have an honest homey quality suggesting the Good Old Days. It's a good idea to remember, though, that a monstrosity a hundred years ago may still be a monstrosity today.

If you don't know what it is, you can always put ivy in it

It's fine advice to buy with brains, not with money alone. Purists also say if you can't use it, don't buy it, no matter how cheap it is, and that wounds auction buffs to the quick, especially those who buy with soul.

Experienced non-professionals understand that if you buy something without knowing what it is (not paying too much for it, of course), it can be a great conversation piece, with everyone speculating on what it was used for originally and what it could be used for now that you're stuck with it.

Buying something for reasons you can't really understand may lead you down a number of un-suspected paths — maybe you'll do a little detective work, tracking down the mystery and starting a new interest. Instead of putting ivy in it, you might identify it and re-create its former atmosphere in a little corner, with your own special ambiance. Adventure can come vicariously when you get an old chest at a country auction and find letters in the drawers.

You may figure out what use another era made of quaint gadgets, or let your imagination blossom for today: old pocket watch cases are fine paper clip holders, sugar shakers look good and are handy for bath powder, toast racks can be used for mail or napkins or guest towel holders, old toothbrush mugs are nice for pencils. People have bought old treadle sewing machines and used their wrought iron sides for balustrades.

Henry Morgan knows how to use what he buys at auction. He bought 100 stained glass windows in one bid and sent them to his friends for Christmas cards.

Are there really any finds?

Truman Capote wrote that one of his great coups in his search for the paperweights he collects was at an auction he wandered into on Long Island. He discovered the prize during the morning exhibition and it didn't come up for sale until late afternoon, during which time he "walked around in a daze of anxiety," wondering if anyone else had an idea of the piece's value. "The auctioneer opened the bidding on the weight at $25, so I knew right away *he* didn't know what he was selling." There was one among the audience who had an inkling that it was something special, but knew very little about it. "When we reached $300 the others in the auditorium began to whisper and stare; they couldn't fathom what it was that made this hunk of glass worth that kind of money. When we arrived at $600 the auctioneer was fairly excited himself, and my rival was sweating; he was having second thoughts, he wasn't really sure. In a faltering voice he bid $650 and I said $700, and that finished him. Afterward, he came over and asked if I thought it was worth $700, and I said, 'No, seven thousand.'"

That's what can happen to a collector who knows what he's doing. Finds for the unknowing are quite rare, although they do happen, like the rare first edition of Hawthorn found at the bottom of a bean pot bought to cook in.

The "mystery package," with its allure of untold riches, is one of the favorite hunting grounds for finds. These are closed containers which can't be inspected in advance and are put up at auctions of household goods or those run by storage companies to dispose of unclaimed merchandise. Bidding on one is high-risk gambling as the numbers or the horses. People have found they've paid twenty or thirty dollars for some carefully packed cracked dishes, or a boxful of left-hand rubber gloves. It's true they have also on occasion found that they've acquired priceless recordings or fine linens or such for a piffling sum. Part of the lure is that valuable goods are known to have been found in such boxes, but nine times out of ten the contents are hardly worth taking away.

His eyes continued to admire the rug, but his nose rebelled. The smell got worse. "Finally," he said, "I realized the rug had been owned by someone with dogs and the dogs had saturated the rug."

The condition of the goods

There are no technical guarantees on the condition of goods sold at auction. Even the finest houses like Parke-Bernet make it a condition of sale that there is no guarantee on the state of the items sold.

Good auctioneers try conscientiously to point out defects, but the buyer assumes the responsibility for looking it over properly first, so that he's aware of any imperfections. "That's a stumbling block to some people, but things are lived with," says a cosmopolitan auctioneer, "and there's likely to be some degree of imperfection. I've gotten to the point where I say everything we offer today has evidence of use. An old chest of drawers, for instance, would invariably have some separated wood, caused by atmospheric conditions."

Other galleries say there is no guarantee as to correctness of description, either. "No sale is set aside, for we cannot be experts in everything. I tell the audience, if you disagree, please do not bid. We are not a retail operation. We sell used merchandise — there is no way we can guarantee it." Their reason: "In certain classes of merchandise I defy so-called experts to authenticate them. Museums are loaded with mistakes. We try to do the best we can within our expertise, with many capable people to help. On the other hand, if we say something is jade or agate or sterling or plate, we guarantee that it is. For repaired or broken things we disclaim all responsibility. Even Parke-Bernet has stopped doing it; you can't help but miss some. Of course, we don't believe in *caveat emptor* — we make people aware of what the piece is and its defects."

Despite the disclaimers of auctioneers, you often have some recourse at reputable establishments. A dealer I know saw a rug at auction that hadn't been listed in the catalogue or put in the exhibition — apparently it had been added at the last minute. He bought it, liked it so much he put it on the floor in his own house. He noticed that it smelled funny, but it was a beautiful rug, not unduly worn, and he was very pleased with his purchase. Maybe the smell was from musty storage and would disappear. His eyes continued to admire the rug, but his nose rebelled. The smell got worse. "Finally," he said, "I realized the rug had been owned by someone with dogs and the dogs had saturated the rug. I took it back. The auctioneer argued, he wasn't very willing, but he finally took it back."

The what-to-buy-in-general bewares

1. Beware the new merchandise made today that looks old.

Many new things are very hard to tell from the old, especially if they're made by the same people who made the originals. Though these are usually sent out with honest labels on them, they can fall into inscrupulous or unaware hands and begin a trail of deception.

Pewter is being made in Holland today, for instance, exactly in the same way it was years ago. They are shipping "antique type" pewter to the U.S. by the ton, some of it well-marked as reproductions.

Gundersen Peachblow glass was very popular in New England during the first part of this century. It's being made again, with honest labels, but

66

today's copy of a former vase is worth about one-tenth the value of the old one it looks exactly like. (Of the new one, a fellow who knows the difference says, "They're probably not going to make any more of this particular style, so it's going up in value soon. I'm going to hang on to it.")

2. Beware two similar items (*not* a pair) being sold one right after the other.

It can happen that the first one is good and goes for a fair price; the second can be a wreck, but if you don't pay attention it might go for close to the same price as the first.

3. Beware not to buy what you can't get through your doorway.

It's very important to measure the space the object is going to occupy and the doorway you're going to have to get it through. First, of course, are you going to be able to get it home from the auction? One fellow says, "It's handy to think about that before you buy something. Finding a $25 piano on your hands after an auction can be upsetting. If the house is for sale, buying it is one solution to this dilemma."

Another solution is to carry a tape measure with you to auctions — and even a magnifying glass (for hallmarks etc.).

4. Beware the new merchandise supposedly being sold at auction to satisfy creditors.

Sometimes this merchandise is made especially to sell at auction (upholstered furniture being one popular item in this category). They're supposedly seconds or "in bankruptcy," but they are really new, especially sold at auction by outfits that hope to benefit from the appeal to bargain hunters.

5. Beware not to buy anything with the idea in mind that you'll fix it up like new.

You won't, unless you're in the fixing business. And don't buy clocks and watches that aren't in good working order—they're very seldom a good buy, for the cost of repairs can be exorbitant.

Sometimes estates include household effects like vacuum cleaners, electric brooms and other appliances. Make sure they work all right, and get a commitment from the auctioneer. I prefer auctioneers like the one I heard announce, "If I say an electric appliance works, you can take that for a guarantee. Bring it back if it doesn't work."

6. Beware of ruining what you buy.

Don't be in a big hurry to paint over something. On an old painted doodad the amount of paint left is important because if it has the original paint or stencil in reasonably good condition, it has more value if left that way. The expert says, "Don't paint old furniture. Get the wood down to the raw—you can't improve on the grain."

7. Beware of those odds-and-ends baskets.

Our farmer friend says, "Examine items before the bidding starts, especially jumbled boxes. Otherwise the auctioneer will wheedle you into buying job lots of mystery cartons that contain nothing more useful than a screwdriver handle, two empty toothpaste tubes, a broken putty gun and a torn copy of *Repairing Horse Harness the Easy Way*."

The auctioneer has to

1. Beware the sneak who slips a valuable piece into a box of trash or mixes a good dish in with some junky ones.

2. Beware the crooks who remove parts of an item up for sale in order to make its price low. This character either points out the deficiency to the auctioneer and buys the article as faulty at a depressed price, or buys it first and then asks for a rebate because of its defect. Or he might notice an interested person at the exhibition and offer to sell him the missing part in case he buys the article (at a bargain price, of course, because of its condition).

The *British Auctioneers' Manual* warns auctioneers who haven't been in practice long to remove keys and pendulums of clocks and other movable articles before the sale. "These appendages are frequently taken," it says, "by the objectionable habitués of the sale . . . who subsequently make overtures to supply the missing parts for a consideration."

A bit about art

One of the smartest auctioneers I ever met says that the trend today is for more and more art of all kinds to be sold over the auction block. "The way manufacturers distribute and merchandise these days you can buy the same toaster any place for approximately the same price. But fine art is singular in being unique and different, each thing in its own individual way."

Americana

Time was when the art had to come from Europe
and be signed by an immortal name to bring
newsworthy prices on the American market. Now
the American masters are getting their licks in. A
growing appreciation for the quality of our own
artists is partly responsible for the leap in prices of
19th and 20th century American works that used to
be the stepchild of art.

A mushrooming nostalgia for the unhurried, civilized
pace of a century ago, plus a new interest in the
romanticism of the 19th century, plays a large part
in the burgeoning market.

American Indian art and artifacts are fast becoming
popular, but hottest right now are paintings from
the Old West. Some of these look like stills from a
grade C movie, though auctioning them, says a
gallery, "is very sedate, never as flamboyant, for
instance, as the Impressionist crowd."

"Folk art" means the primitive or naive paintings
produced by American folk painters in the early
days of our country. Some experts feel it's a pity
that education and the influence of Europe should
have "altered the natural talent of our early artists
and made them all conventional, because, alone
and untutored, they expressed themselves delight-
fully." Others feel this style simply reflected an
ignorance of traditional painting.

A painting can look like a genuine primitive or a
19th century romantic work and sell for less than
$50, and actually be completely genuine. There are
genuine pictures that seem to have been executed

70

What manner of man is this—
"What a ham!" Some auctioneers
are smoother than others, but
they're all actors. And they have
to play varying roles without the
lines a playwright provides an
actor.

by a one-armed house painter with a severe tic, for there is bad art as well as good. Which doesn't mean that if it's cheap it's no good. What it means is that if you're not an expert, just buy what you like and can afford, and the devil with whether you've got a find. Don't be sucked in by the little inner voice that says, "It might be a real Czktchznyw! bid more, more!" Experts say smart people buy out of love, and ten years later if they find they have a windfall they never expected — so much to the good.

Whether it's prints or paintings or sculpture or whatever, try to buy the genuine and shop for quality. Those who know say, "Fame and quality often coincide, but not always. The person buying primarily for quality, *regardless of the label,* will find that there are still bargains to be had, even in the field of so-called Old Masters."

Victorian art

Today's glamour girl can turn into tomorrow's outcast any time, and today's Cinderella may one day be recognized as a princess. Victorian art is an example. Victorian painters were highly paid in their own lifetimes, reaching a peak of wealth and fame in the 1890s. With the new century, the tide turned, and it ended in complete ebb in the 1930s. Fashionable critics ridiculed the work of the Victorians as sentimental story-telling and it became regarded automatically as inferior. Even up to about 1950 people who bought any kind of Victorian painting were thought of at least as eccentric.

Now, many of the big names in Victorian art have already risen out of reach of the average buyer, but there is still something for every taste and every pocket. There's no telling if that tide will turn back again, or rise even higher, which is another reason to buy only what will give you pleasure to look at.

The art bewares

1. Beware that insidious planting device, also used at art auctions.

It's the tactic of mixing substandard or unauthentic works with those that are obviously valuable, for the purpose of enhancing the value of the no-goods. One of my rural informants says in disgust, "They get 25 name paintings, see, and then 50 more from students or dabblers trying to make a buck, and they sell real good, mixed up with the 25 name paintings."

In officialese, "If the intent is to mislead buyers rather than simply to combine items for efficient sales purposes, such action is illegal."

2. Beware the copies.

There are remarkable copies of paintings in existence, most of them not originally painted to deceive. But it has been proved discouragingly that even the world's great art experts are not infallible and fakes hanging in museums are constantly being discovered.

Early in this century, a famous French collector had four Turners, three of which he knew very well were fakes (he had paid a few dollars for them, grudgingly, and several thousand for the authentic one). A dealer who knew him well wrote, "He presented one fake to the Louvre for the fun of seeing it hung there by the curators, who hoped he would bequeath them his collection. And he let them go on thinking it. He didn't leave them as much as one drawing, so a few days after his funeral they had the fake Turner taken down, but then they began having hopes for his widow, and rehung it."

3. Beware the deceptive restoration.

It drastically reduces the value of the work of art, however great the artist. Some things are skillfully restored without intention to deceive, but sooner or later they may fall into the possession of an amateur who is deluded into believing he owns a flawless original work.

4. Beware the "run-up" on work of contemporary artists.

The gallery who represents the artist has a vested interest in getting high prices for his client's work. They often put something up for auction with a high reserve on it. If they don't get a "live" bidder, they bid it in themselves (by proxy) and even pay the commission — it's worth it to them, for they use that as negotiating base for a future sale of that painting, as well as others by the same artist. This works in smaller ways for jacking up prices on lesser known artists of which the gallery or collector has a goodly supply he'd like to get rid of.

Good auction houses try to prevent this, but there isn't much they can do. However, to discourage it they have begun to reveal to the press which works of art were "bought in." In London they include the buyer's name on the price list, which makes it more difficult for such "prices" to look legitimate.

5. Beware of falling for fads.

Many artists who were making big news and big money in the past few years "suddenly no longer look old master, just old hat," says one critic. "The proud owners of their work inexplicably find it expendable. Can it be to raise needed money that these millionaire collectors have consigned to auction flocks of not yesterday's but just this morning's big names?"

Stick to the top auction galleries to help protect yourself against inflated prices and even frauds. Don't be afraid of the swank houses—Parke-Bernet, for example, doesn't usually sell art works under $100 (although you never know what can happen), but at least 60 percent of all lots auctioned by them go for less than $250.

Prints

Prints are wonderful things to have. They open up new possibilities of acquiring original works of art, they're small, they're usually inexpensive, and they can be very soul-satisfying, all good reasons for their rising popularity. The desire for original prints has become so widespread that some contemporary artists are putting out more than sixty editions a year. That's a lot of prints, but the print bugs are eating them up.

The word "prints" takes in a number of techniques: woodcut, lino-cut, engraving, drypoint, etching, lithograph, serigraph. It isn't necessary to know the details of each kind to enjoy a good print, but it helps, and it isn't hard to find out. For instance, it's nice to know that an engraving is a design cut into a metal plate with ink rubbed into the incised lines, which are then printed under pressure. For an etching the incisions in the plate are made with chemicals. Of course, there's much more to the technical processes than that, and to know something about them leads to seeing how they affect the final result: the kind of line obtained, the planes, the background, the shading, all the finer points that make prints good.

Although there are prints that cost $50,000, 90 percent of all the prints ever created could probably be bought for under $275 apiece, and there are quality originals going from $20 to $50. Black and white prints are the least expensive.

Some of the fertile but not yet fully appreciated fields for fine prints are said by the cognoscenti to be: almost all the lesser names in 16th and 17th century art; European and American artists of the 1920's; German Expressionists; the Ashcan school and the Barbizon school, who are "19th century artists still extraordinarily inexpensive compared to the name artists of the 20th century."

The print bewares

1. Beware, warn the experts, of signed reproductions.

They are not original prints and although they may go for several hundred dollars, "they are virtually valueless."

2. Beware of such misleading labels as Rouault, Clowns, lithograph, original limited edition.

That description doesn't really say anything, and sidesteps committing itself on authenticity.

3. Beware that the signature, if any, is authentic.

The signature can make this kind of difference: I have seen an unsigned Picasso print go for $20, while its identical counterpart, signed, went for $310. The aesthetic value was the same for both. Whether the print is numbered, however, doesn't make all that difference, because not all artists number their prints.

4. Beware what you do with the print after you've bought it.

It should be framed by an expert, because improper mounting can lower its value. If you leave it unframed, it should be put into a portfolio for protection.

5. Beware the restrike.

It is an original print, but it's the result of an etched plate that remains in existence long after the death of the artist, and its continued use might be producing works that would make the artist turn over in his grave.

Beware what certain auctioneers call "various selling techniques," better defined as the old shell game.

5

BUYING ANTIQUES AT AUCTION

Antiques from everywhere surface in the auction rooms. Besides art and furniture of all kinds, there are tapestries, chandeliers, rugs, lamps, candelabra, statues, snuffboxes, chess sets, stucco and ivory reliefs, urns, books, coins, photographs, porcelain and pottery, arms and armor, musical instruments, tankards and teapots and silver ships, jewelry—the list could go on forever. There are memorabilia like "Baby's Bottle in green leather case lined in purple velvet from which the Duc de Nemours (born 1814) was suckled;" and "Mounted Specimen of an extinct Great Auck, taken c. 1821 from Iceland."

We Americans are great consumers. Since we also consume other countries' antiques and artifacts, we're accused of looting Europe of its treasure with American money. It so happens we're just the latest in a long line of antique hunters. It started farther back than 2300 years ago, when Alexander the Great's Greek soldiers ("still smelling of goat," according to the aristocrats of conquered Persia) snatched up the Persians' treasures.

Later it was the Greeks who complained about the Romans buying up Greek treasures, and using Greek experts to advise them on top of it. Then it was the turn of the Romans, along with the Florentines, to watch the French remove their masterpieces and folk art; when the French needed money it was the English who bought their art objects and removed them to their own country. Now the English are complaining about Americans bidding for what the English consider their national treasure, non-English objects included.

Definitions

Most people call anything made the day before yesterday an antique. As long as it was made before their time, it must be antique.

U.S. Customs says antiques are any objects 100 years old or more. The U.S. Government, however, (which one would think would be on intimate terms with its Customs laws) rules that anything is an antique which was made before 1830. That particular cut-off date is when machines started to mass produce articles which till then had been made by craftsmen's hands.

"As far as the antique stuffed shirts are concerned," dissents a critic, "1830 represents the end of artistic achievements and the beginning of artistic bankruptcy, a perfectly absurd position."

For instance, most carved Victorian pieces are technically antiques, but they were cut by power machine and mass produced by pattern. Excellent Hitchcock chairs were factory-made but had hand-turned detail.

Some antiqueniks (of which there seem to be no end in this country) say that an antique doesn't have to have beauty or grace or charm—its essence is to tell something of the roots of our culture; antiques go to the sources of who we are. Then the country auctioneer grumbles about "heirs who think that because they've found something carved and faded and dusty in grandmother's barn or attic, they've found something of antique value."

As you can see, there is no agreement whatsoever on what is antique, and a certain degree of acerbity attends the discussion. To cut through the confusion, let's accept that antiques are anything in our culture that reminds us of a way of life different from our present one.

Styles

There have been hundreds of books written about antiques, so if you are interested in learning about them or in a particular kind of antiques, the best place is the public library. What I can give you here are some general ideas that might provide a little insight into this interest that is burgeoning like roses under a June sun.

Don't be discouraged by the endless chaos of terminology—simple general designation is good enough. There aren't any sharp dividing lines between style periods anyway. For instance, the Federal period in France ran from about 1781 to 1815; the next period was called Empire (when Napoleon took over) and you'd think, therefore, it would have started in 1816. It didn't. There was a blurring and blending of designs; potters and painters and furniture-makers moved constantly from place to place; the center of style change was in the city, and country furniture was always about 50 years behind.

One of the most widely used style names is Victorian, which takes its name from the Queen and covers the years of her reign (1837–1901). Actually the style was a direct steal from the French, particularly Victorian Rococo (featuring masses of curves and carving) and the Victorian Renaissance (out with the curves and on with the carving). There are about six different Victorian period styles, the last of which was called Turkish, from which came all those inflated overstuffed pieces, as well as the ubiquitous fringe that decorated every possible edge.

Hepplewhite is another name frequently dropped by antiquers. Some historians doubt that George Hepplewhite ever had a furniture shop, let alone designed furniture. Nevertheless, for many years now the antique market has recognized a particular style as Hepplewhite.

Take Chippendale as another example. One fellow tells about buying something at auction labeled "true Chippendale." He says, "it wasn't antique, it wasn't English, and it wasn't mahogany. It was made in 1860 by some clever American cabinetmaker. How do I know? It looked like mahogany, but it was redwood—you could tell by the grain and by your fingernail, as it was softer than mahogany— and we didn't use redwood until the West opened up. But it was true Chippendale. Chippendale was a designer (as well as a cabinetmaker) who published many books. When you refer to a Chippendale, you refer to a style, and a true Chippendale is a true style. A piece of furniture made in the Chippendale shops is practically unknown here. In the same way Sheraton also means only a style."

You've probably had people show you their Sèvres china. Well, there's Sèvres and there's Sèvres. The original was made for Louis XV and specimens of it were given by him to ambassadors, kings, noble relatives, and mistresses. The secret formula for this soft-paste china was destroyed in 1804, and later a hard-paste process was used. Some of it was embellished by copies of the old ornaments, via hydrochloric acid etching, and sold as true old Sèvres. "Even worse," says the expert, "there is a cheap French imitation, gaudy plates of which have been sold at large sums to people with more money than brains. There are also several excellent French imitations which find a ready American market."

Americana

There are infinitely more foreign-made antiques available here than native antiques. Early American antiques are much more valuable than imported ones, and always will be, because of their rarity.

American cabinetmakers like Duncan Phyfe copied European styles such as Queen Anne and Georgian, but the Americans also developed their own unique variations. They tended toward the simple and the utilitarian, partly a heritage of Puritanism and partly a practical conservation of energy and materials.

Eighteenth-century American furniture and silver are particularly important to antiquers because they were made by American craftsmen, in contrast to the porcelain and glass of the times which were largely imported. Good 18th-century furniture of the better sort, made with loving care by

Yankee craftsmen, is expensive, much sought after and not easy to find. But there are still ample supplies of simpler, less expensive country pieces, tangible links to the past even if they do lack the sophistication of old Newport or Salem.

The kinds of things antiquers like are endless, and some of them will buy anything, regardless of what it is. How would you like an ale shoe? It was a metal vessel resembling a shoe horn and used to heat ale in the fireplace.

Or how about a lapdesk? They came into use around 1820, before central heating, when you brought your desk with you to the fireplace, and for many years thereafter they were very popular and plentiful. Today they are quite cheap to buy, but I haven't figured out how useful. You can get a nice horse collar for quite a low bid at many auctions—never mind what you are going to do with it. An oldtimer talks about another star of the summer circuit: "Old lobster traps," he says, "worn out but intact. Very attractive. Smell of the sea. Romantic looking, bleached wood." So? But if you see someone bidding tenaciously for old snapshots of strangers in an old picture album that looks like trash, don't think he's lost his mind—he may be a clever collector who wants the very valuable revenue stamps on the back.

Learning

To intelligently bid on antique furniture takes a great deal of knowledge and experience. There's a lot to watch for at exhibitions, such as the wooden dowel pins, for instance, which in antiques are many sided, not round. If they're perfectly round

It's nice to develop a discerning eye. With practice you'll be able to recognize good workmanship and design, and then work up to the fine points.

you know they're machine made. Or the dovetails, where the front of a drawer is fitted into the sides, and which were crude in early pieces, sometimes two inches wide each. American 18th century and 19th century dovetails were about one inch wide and uniform, there usually being three of them. Modern dovetails are small and frequent.

Experts have to know dozens of things like that, and they have to have enough solid experience to know the real article from the fake. But there is a way of judging for non-experts—not on names and value, but just for personal use. You can develop an eye for design, a feeling for color, a style of your own. Inborn good taste helps a lot, but when you go to an auction, you can learn by actual handling. Watch for the sound of a glass, for weight, the feel in your hands, the mellowness of color. Keep your eye peeled for beauty of workmanship and finish, for the execution of an object: stitches, carving, brushwork.

Exercise your intuition. To get a general impression of an object as a whole, step far enough away and look through squinted eyes at the whole thing at one time. Does it hang together well? Is the design pleasing? Are its lines graceful and its proportions good (are the feet right for the rest of it, is the top too heavy or the bottom too thick)?

An oldtimer gives this advice in learning about styles: "Manufacturers keep their ear to the ground and are quick to sense a demand—their goods are sold in stores as new reproductions, so keep your eyes open on them. It's not only a good way to learn, but to recognize them when these repro-duced items end up in antique sales."

"Ask questions," says the auctioneer. "A legitimate auction house doesn't mind. For two years we had a lady in here asking questions, almost a pest, she asked so many, but they were answered. She's developed perfect taste. Everything she buys is good. We prefer the knowledgeable buyer—they get full value because they know what things are worth."

Another adviser says, "Come to the exhibition and learn. It's like going to class." Auctions are great places to learn as long as you hold back on bidding. You can teach yourself at them by taking notes, writing down the items and your opinions of them, as well as what they bring. This helps you to develop a sixth sense that will reinforce your judgment.

Go to the auction and look look look. Feel with your hands, educate your eyes.

Where all those antiques come from

Antiques come, says a knowledgeable old curmudgeon who has personally covered all of North America in his quest, from: the rural areas of the New England states, and then, in descending order of importance, from New York, New Jersey, Pennsylvania, Ohio, North Carolina, and Georgia. "Not the big cities, where the antiques have already passed through several hands, the prices rising each time." As for antiques in the rest of the country—what he calls the migration states— "75% of them were hauled there from the original states, and I don't mean by covered wagon, either, but in some antique dealer's station wagon. In the case of Texas, I'd raise the figure to 90 percent."

From the Chinese came a great deal of the china ware Americans used early in the 19th century. Most of what the Chinese made for export was based on what they assumed Americans preferred, although they managed, fortunately, to keep the simplicity Orientals have always favored.

One of the giants in the history of glass making, Joseph Locke, came to America from England and was much honored for his craftsmanship. In the field of china, Haviland was started originally in New York, but when the owner recognized within a few years that Americans favored French china, he started his own factory at Limoges, France, and exported it to America.

The sources of our antiques are as varied as the rainbow-splotched glassware known as Carnival glass, a much-prized genre today that came by its name because it was used as carnival prizes for knocking some poor fellow off his perch and into the water with a baseball.

Looking for authenticity

It's nice to develop a discerning eye. With practice you'll be able to recognize good workmanship and design, and then work up to the fine points. People who buy antique furniture say they examine anything they're interested in very carefully, pulling out drawers, tipping it up to see if it has the original legs or feet or handles.

There are more things to check on than you can shake a stick at, and it is possible to learn some of them, for instance certain signs of age. When you see a chair with the legs worn down so much that the stretchers are near the floor, that comes from use, and is especially evident in the very old chairs that were pulled around on the dirt floors of early taverns. There might be worn front stretchers from generations of feet hooked over them.

You can tell if a round table is antique because a mark of its age will be revealed by measuring it—if it's old it will have shrunk some with the years and measure slightly less in diameter across the grain than with it.

You might not be able to tell old Queen Anne from new, but you could acquire useful knowledge (and a variety of splinters) from looking at drawers. A plywood bottom on a drawer means it's a modern replacement. The interiors of old drawers were never shellacked or varnished. Their under-sides were planed by hand and you can feel uneven ridges and hollows with your hands. The lower edge of an old drawer as it slides out shows the curve of wear from thousands of openings and closings.

Repair is not necessarily a bad word. A repaired piece is not, of course, worth as much as the same thing in mint condition, but there wouldn't be much available without repaired things. Glorification is a bad word. That's when a simple thing has been gussied up to fool you, or a repaired piece is offered as an original. Rebuilt is usually in the same class as glorified. That's when a few pieces of one or more old wrecks are assembled into a so-called antique.

The customs ruling that articles 100 years old or more are admitted free of duty also states that an antique must be of the original material, with only sufficient repairs justified by its age. Much restored furniture sold as antique doesn't come up to that standard, so unless you're an expert, what matters is if you like it and get it for a price you feel is fair. Another pertinent law passed in 1892 says that all merchandise imported into the U.S. had to be marked with its country of origin. Therefore, a hallmark (identifying sign like an impressed emblem on the back) that says *"made in . . . ,"* means that item was made after 1892 and is not, technically, an antique—yet.

Honest reproductions

There is now no article of 18th century furniture in any wood, any style, or in any form that cannot be purchased as a reproduction, all made openly and above board. Beautiful reproductions of all kinds are manufactured under license, some are made by hand, and all of these are properly marked as reproductions. The old chair factory of Lambert Hitchcock is once more being used for its original purpose and making perfect replicas of its old chairs. Experts say Hitchcock himself never did a better job, and each chair comes signed with his old stencil along with its reproduction mark.

Whenever there is a fine, valid piece there will be good reproductions (some of the reproductions themselves are over 100 years old, and even current ones will some day enjoy their own antiquehood). Williamsburg Reproductions are so marked and are famous. Their handmade cinnamon shaker, for instance, is made the same way delft was made in colonial days, and to make sure that no one mistakes any for the original they bake the date of manufacture into the piece.

The manufacturer of "French Blue Milk Glass," made from old molds, advertises that they're an exciting revival of great old favorites. Just don't buy them as antiques.

One should be careful, however, because there are reproductions of everything. Note how reproductions are just too good, they're not repaired or rickety, they have no irregularities. If you aren't a connoisseur, don't attempt to buy genuine, expensive antiques without the advice of an expert, and never from someone whom you're not going to be able to find next week or next month. Just bid on the comparatively inexpensive items without pedigree that you like, want to use, and which may or may not turn out some day to be valuable.

Snakery fakery

An old antique buff said long ago that all that is decrepit is not antique. In dear old London they are making decrepitude while you wait.

"Authentic" is defined as something that was manufactured and used in the period represented. Anything knowingly misrepresented as to age, maker, condition, history, and style, is a fake. There isn't an expert who won't admit that even he can be fooled or confused. There was a case of a well-known antique dealer who was called in by customs to rule on a shipment of tapestry held in their warehouse. His verdict: modern. Two months later, not knowing that he was on the same case, he declared the same lot to be rare antiques.

The best the non-expert can do is arm himself against crude frauds at high prices. Many of the

"Your palms begin to sweat, you can feel your face getting red, your heart begins to pound, and you cannot stop." It may sound like love, but it's auction fever.

deliberate fakes placed in circulation have been created by men who know just as much or more about them than the men who finally judge them. Ordinarily it doesn't pay to fake inexpensive stuff, except perhaps for the low-end snake oil salesman who throws away the labels on pottery that say "made in Japan," and substitutes "hand-made in Portugal" or "Italy" — and he eventually gets caught at it. Fakes are generally found only in high-priced items. But the faker wants none of the extremely high market either, for that brings the experts sniffing around. It is financial suicide to fake some things. Most Victorian furniture, with all those scrolls and curlicues and heavy walnut boards, would cost at least twice their going price to fake. The fakes it pays to make have no intricate carving or veneer, and no large inner surfaces that have to be made to look antique. Profitable fakes would be items like a Hepplewhite card table or Pembroke tables or early Butterfly tables, which could then be sold for very handsome prices. Of course, scholars and experts often debate a long time after one faction declares a fake, and some of the condemned objects are eventually cleared.

Made in Europe

Our expert on fakes says, "For every fake made in America, 100 have been produced abroad: in England, France, Italy, Holland, Scandinavia. Nothing is too mediocre to attract European fakers as long as there is money in the deal. Part of the story is that the principal market for European-made fakes is America."

That is nothing new. Europe has been busy with counterfeiting for a long time. In 1921 an antiquer wrote, "Italy, particularly around Florence, is doing a rushing trade in furniture with every indication of antiquity craftily manifest. And near Versailles there is a colony of tapestry weavers who are catering to the demand for Gothics (sic) by altering less saleable pieces and interweaving Gobelins animals and birds."

The current fakers in Italy who have been exporting false Etruscan antiquities around the world (which have been found in all kinds of collections, including the Metropolitan Museum) are much appreciated by their government. "It's better to see fake art leave the country than our artistic patrimony," a high official says. "We consider the fakers almost our collaborators." Imitation Etruscan art is big business, with factories and display tombs and a $30 million annual turnover. They say they're performing a public service—just in case you're offered any Etruscan antiquities.

An antique dealer in Turkey was summoned to court for offering antiques to customers before submitting them to museum authorities. The police found, among other things, "four marble busts of rare workmanship, a small statue of Cybele and a beautiful Greek vase, perfectly preserved, a masterpiece of workmanship." The dealer did not seem perturbed. "Most of them were fake anyway," he said.

Oh well, fakes go back to 8th century B.C. Greece. Potters then were copying beautiful Corinthian vases and faking the signatures of the better known artisans. Phaedrus wrote in 15 B.C., "Sculptors carved the name of Praxiteles (born 3 centuries earlier) on their marbles and the name of Myron on everything they wrought in silver."

94

It's still considered a miracle in New Bedford, Massachusetts, that when the whaleship Charles W. Morgan went to sea it didn't sink in the harbor— considering the number of harpoons that have since been sold from it.

Some of the fakes to watch out for

Don't be taken in by pasted-on pieces of dated old newspapers. And never mind being impressed by pegged wood. Grand Rapids is still using wooden pegs on certain pieces of furniture. Don't fall for the so-called sea chests, which actually were the kind of chests carpenters used to leave on the job around 1910. As heavy as lead with thick, heavy inset metal handles, they certainly were not carried on board ship.

The fakes expert says "under the name of Dresden and Meissen crimes have been committed. Great masses of this ware have been placed on the market at various times, some of it clever enough to call for the expert's magnifying glass and some of it crude enough to be detected from across the room."

Dresden is a generic term. Meissen was where Royal Saxony pottery was made. "After both World Wars the American army lugged home a considerable amount of 'Dresden' that came from the busy factory of a Mme. Wolfsohn in Dresden." When the German government sued it, this enterprising outfit switched the hallmark and valiantly carried on feeding the hungry maw of the American market. The deluded people who think they are buying 'Dresden' don't know that the famous clay pits in Meissen to which this china owed its beauty, gave out long before World War I."

As for antique Worcester, Lowestoft, Staffordshire, Delft, and Wedgwood, the deceptions range from crude Japanese and German fakes funneled through American warehouses, to a grandiose nervy scheme of one Mr. Samson in Paris. Close your ears to blandishments, dear readers, and keep your bids low. In 1909 an American consul in England wrote home: "Dresden, Worcester and Chelsea are worth more than their weight in gold, yet what one may fondly imagine to be a convincing piece is a fake made by a well-known firm on the Continent. Literally tons of faked Sheffield plate are now being manufactured, most of which, sooner or later, finds its way to America and the colonies."

The hanky-panky that goes on with silver is sad indeed. Fortunes are made because some clever villain can take genuine old hallmarks from badly damaged pieces and neatly solder them into modern reproductions. Other crooks just forge hallmarks. Not only do they call anything that is silver plate over copper (or over anything) Sheffield, they often include the electroplating process (EPNS) in their claims. And something marked "Genuine Sheffield" or "Genuine pewter" is like something marked "Genuine antique."

Another common fraud is with the ubiquitous Sandwich glass Dolphin candlesticks, of which imitations are manufactured in the thousands. On the antique one, the component parts were fused by hand after they came from the mold, and the alignment, therefore, between the mold seam in the body of the dolphin and the panel seam in the candleholder was usually off. Imitations come from a completely finished mold and the alignment is perfect.

96

There seems to be nothing these dastardly characters won't turn their hand to—even antique wireless sets are being brewed in their basements and garages. Some wisenheimer with an old mold for casting iron roosters ages them by salting them down and leaving them out in the weather to rust properly. Two of these forgeries are said to now decorate outstanding restored historical homes.

Don't think all fakes are new. Plenty were made 50 years ago. Some imitations eventually come to be valued by the same principle that make book or stamp collectors value "errors." Others, like Wedgwood's copies of the famous ancient Portland vase, are valuable collector's items. And we can all be thankful for Rubens' copy of the painting of Isabella d'Este by Titian, which preserves the memory of the lost original.

The antique bewares

1. Beware the will to believe, which can also be very strong.

Thirty years ago when a leading auctioneer was first learning about antiques, he saw a 19th century Chippendale dining room table he wanted at an auction sale in Connecticut. "Even though I saw on it an electric bell push, I wanted that table to be what it was supposed to be, and I made myself believe it was. I knew a real one couldn't have an electric bell push, but I talked myself into buying it."

Around the time of World War I an old auction buff wrote that most people are satisfied if they think something is old. All they need is to find a page from something old pasted over the bottom of some drawer, and there's the evidence of authenticity they need. "It certainly is good psychology, and some fellows plant these around as if they were salting a mine. It's so easy to get old documents, worthless for anything else—old legal papers dumped out of offices by the barrowful."

A good convincer is a bit of history, like a letter signed in wobbly hand by great-aunt Matilda telling how General "Brick" Wilkinson visited her grand-daddy and rocked on the porch in this very chair. The letter is written in rusty ink (modern aging method), and the paper is brittle and yellowed (until recently it was the flyleaf of a worthless old book).

An old down-easter once wrote, "A small piece of china two inches high and three inches wide, by itself of negligible interest, might be used either as an aquarium ornament or to throw at a howling cat. However, the whole situation is put in a different light by a few words: 'That,' the auc-tioneer remarks, taking a long breath and shifting onto his strong leg, 'was inherited by the nephew of Senator Gargle who got it from his father-in-law who found it while privateering off the Isle of Man. Do I hear $25?' ($25 is the standard starting price for small articles with histories)."

2. Beware of the two most popular names for old glass—the only two kinds many auctioneers seem to know of—Stiegel and Sandwich.

One professional says he doesn't think one percent of the Stiegel glass on the market was ever made by Stiegel. As for Sandwich glass, the real, old Sand-wich glass was made before 1888 in clear or 'lacy' pieces. Later, most of the real Sandwich glass was made in the 1890s and sold to tea dealers to give away as premiums. There's so little to distinguish it from that of dozens of other factories, it takes a very knowledgeable expert.

As an example of putting too much store in names, a judge who was a famous collector once wrote, "While I was convinced that my enameled glasses were made by Baron Stiegel, they were, I thought, beautiful. But when I recognized that Baron Stiegel had not made them, they immediately, in my eyes, became ugly." It can't be true, said an antiquer who learned the hard way, that Baron Stiegel only had a tiny place and produced his glass during a very few years. From the amount of genuine Stiegel bought, the baron's factory must have been the size of the Ford plant and worked a 24-hour shift for at least 50 years.

3. Beware to protect yourself in the clinches.

Hold china up to the light to spot mended breaks or imperfections. Rub your fingers over glass edges for chips, or ground-down chips. Watch out for anachronisms, like a set of cut glass old-fashioneds, very few of which could go back to the cut glass era. Be sure of true mates, the right stopper, the right accompanists such as pulls on furniture, bottles in a cruet stand.

4. Beware to examine any object you want to bid on first, carefully, and question the auctioneer.

If the auctioneer won't tell you what you need to know, go to someone else's sales. If you ask him is it old, and he shrugs and says something like "It could be," put it down and forget it.

5. Beware of the condition of the article.

For instance, cloudiness in glass (called sick glass); stains; weak impress design; age cracks (called crazing on dishes, crizzling in glass and checking in paint) which are a minute irregular network of hairlines caused in antique plates by repeated warmings in brick ovens or on wood burning cookstoves (or in my dishwasher).

In old silver, pewter or brass, however, "minute scratches and small dents bespeak genuineness." Note their sheen—new shine shows as new; only age and repeated polishing give an old patina sheen.

Note especially spouts of teapots, handles on cream pitchers, hands of figurines and such easily broken appendages. Hold them up to the light to see if they've been repaired with filler. But if you like it anyway, point it out to the auctioneer *beforehand* so he'll have to call attention to the defect during the auction.

6. Beware the multitude of so-called Staffordshire figurines that are made in Czechoslovakia and Japan.

These fakes are not clean cut; their poor colors are carelessly applied with a rough or crude glaze; any gold or lustre stripes are garishly bright.

7. Beware of pitted metal objects.

Such corrosion is uncorrectable and reduces the value of a piece by 3/4. Sick pewter has an oxidation of the alloy which is not just on the surface, but has penetrated so deeply it can't be removed, and makes the piece valueless.

8. Beware the auctioneer who consistently says "I believe this is," or "You've had a chance to examine." He's the one who boasts "I let the customer be his own expert," and I wouldn't buy $1 bills from him for a quarter.

Ask yourself if the auctioneer said "This is (marble; Lowestoft; early 19th century; perfect; etc.) or did he say "This could be . . . ," or "it has been described as . . ." If he says "Imari style" or anything-*style,* that is a tacit indication that it's not rated as an antique.

Each auction firm has its own way of rating the authenticity of a particular work. Sotheby's, for example, might rate a painting attributed to Sir Joshua Reynolds as Sir Joshua Reynolds, P. R. A. (highly confident of its authenticity); Sir J. Reynolds (probably authentic but not positive); or simply Reynolds (caution indicated).

The Collector—What makes people want to own things they don't need? Answers range from a desire to "hand down the tangible remnants of civilization" to "collecting is a disease," or a "reasonable solution to the problem of being gainfully but unhappily employed."

6

COLLECTING

"The collectors are not just the Whitneys, the Rockefellers, and the Chryslers any more. They've been joined by thousands of people, young lawyers, dentists, and doctors who have done well in their professions, business men, media people." — A Parke-Bernet Vice President.

There is a difference between collecting and accumulating. The accumulator might be an obsessive junk hunter, with no particular objective. Only when he begins to discriminate, narrow his interest down to specific items, does he graduate into the collector class, new collectors must study their specialty; they'd also be wise to make the acquaintance of a reputable auctioneer or antiquary, and to solicit his advice. Auctioneers are quite fond of collectors because, they say, they know value and offset rings.

All auction buffs certainly aren't collectors, but all collectors do frequent auctions. Auctions are usually the only place where they can buy single pieces from someone else's collection and, at the same time, save themselves a lot of the work the previous owner had to go through, for collections are not put together overnight; they require a healthy measure of time and effort — in addition to money.

The collector

What makes people want to own things they don't
need? Answers range from a desire to "hand down
the tangible remnants of civilization" to "collecting
is a disease," or a "reasonable solution to the
problem of being gainfully but unhappily employed."

Big-time collectors are said to enjoy a psychic
income — prestige and ego satisfaction — but they
have other motives as well. According to the
president of America's greatest auction firm,
collectors buy "for investment, for snobbish reasons,
or for personal immortality gained by buying
something and donating it to a museum."

At home, the collector is probably gentle and
kindly, but on the trail of a rare piece at an auction
he can turn suddenly ferocious. An auctioneer in
the mid-West told me, "Collectors have no allegiance
to anyone. They're fanatics. Collectors of fine art are
a very unusual breed — very odd, never average.
They're eccentric because they're collectors, not the
other way around. Often his home is a museum, an
institution instead of a home."

The director of the famous Frick Collection spoke
of the "gnawing obsessions, stealthy pursuits,
crushing disappointments, and intoxicating triumphs"
felt by the collector. A novice confesses the activity
provides "the excitement of a new love affair.
The collector must have a touch of madness . . .
his world is a world by itself, full of beauty and
hope in which the anticipation of each new object
is an adventure which grips him to the depths every
time."

The collecting nut is easy to recognize at an exhibition. He fondles an object in the manner peculiar to glass experts; having rubbed it against his cheek, touched it with his tongue and his nose, felt the pontil mark, and otherwise tested it, he issues his evaluation.

Extremes of high passion and low motive may touch the average, small-time collector occasionally, but ordinarily he attends auctions to satisfy a curiosity, exercise a detective instinct, engage in stimulating competition. If he bids successfully for an object, he may feel a sensuous pleasure in owning it. Touching it, savoring its smell, detail, and distinctive qualities brings joy every time. It doesn't have to be the rarest procelain or the most delicate tapestry — it just has to be what he likes.

The mystery of the auction is a masked marvel called the Anonymous Private Collector, "about whose multiple identity the art world loves to speculate. Alone in some secluded chamber, snifter and cigar in hand, Mr. APC is no doubt gazing at a chef d'oeuvre that is now his, and his alone, and relishing the thrill of conquest."

The collectibles

Just as collectors no longer are found only in the upper classes, collectibles no longer are limited to rare and costly relics of the past. Some of the things collected are baffling, but what enthusiast can understand another? The person who collects old thumb latches regards with pity his brother collector of early fountain pens, who in turn believes that the man who collects Dutch marriage certificates is odd but not necessarily dangerous, while the collector of wooden sap buckets and early American hairbrushes is in need of immediate attention by a psychiatrist.

Everyone has his reason for choosing whatever it is he collects. One person may decide to make a collection for use as home decoration. Another may value objects with historical significance. You could make a collection for sentimental or romantic reasons, or for tie-ins with your profession (like an architect who collects old tools, or a doctor who collects old apothecary jars).

If you enjoy poking around auctions, and would like to start a collection but don't wish to spend too much money, you can settle on something like pressed glass footwear, sometimes known as "early Woolworth"; or "antiques of the future," like calendars, perfume bottles, compacts, defunct maps, wine labels, old greeting cards, college pennants. All these things turn up at small auctions. If you want to spend a little more on a collection, you can choose old hat pins, or their holders, potty figures, old pewter Victoriana, buttonhooks, old trivets, door markers, sleighbells, Wedgwood Jasperware, music boxes; or objects from a certain time period, such as the years of World War I or the second half of the 1940s or the Depression years.

The objects available to collect really seem endless. What you must do is fix on a subject, preferably not too large or expensive, yet interesting to you—old hitching posts, barber poles, keys, muffin stands, napkin rings, painted trays, pin cushions, hooked rugs, or even pink cups. And of course, you can always progress. If you collect canning jars, for instance, and find that isn't a big enough challenge, you can always start out in pursuit of the more elusive old canning jar funnels.

Many people collect local items, like pieces of wood from the trees from which various people were hanged, or bullets to which ghastly murders are connected, or packages of dirt from disaster sites. In the West, where a hundred years ago there was a pressing fencing problem, there are now 150,000 collectors of barbed wire.

The items collectors are looking for are varied and often strange. They include: anything pertaining to President Millard Fillmore; old orange juice squeezers; OPA items; thermometers; World War I posters for Liberty Bonds and recruitment; Shirley Temple glassware; wind-up phonographs and early crystal radios; decoys—ducks, geese, and crows; • tennis memorabilia; old cash registers; radio show premiums; and frosted lions (whatever those are).

Comic books of the thirties, forties, and fifties are big collectors' items now, but the "penny dreadful" has been popular with collectors since before the World War I. The penny dreadful was "a flimsy pamphlet cheaply concocted for appetites that craved more of the gruesome morbid details in a crime case than the daily newspapers supplied." An 1885 penny dreadful was entitled *A Confession of the Awful and Bloody Transactions in the Life of Charles Wallace, the Fiendlike Murderer of Miss Mary Rogers, Beautiful Cigar Girl of Broadway.*

There are collectors who curse themselves for throwing away their bubble gum cards of yesteryear and spend a lot of time watching for somone else to throw away theirs. Serious collectors of bubble gum cards spend hundreds of dollars on them. Cards of baseball figures that used to be issued with cigarettes are also in demand: One collector bid $1000 for a Honus Wagner card that was distributed in 1910 with packages of Sweet Caporal cigarettes. That particular card was a rarity because the great shortstop, who didn't want his name connected with tobacco, threatened to sue, and Sweet Caporal withdrew most of the cards from the market.

The collectible doesn't have to be so old before collectors or memorabilia rush in. During their heyday, blimps were immortalized in pewter and tin as ice cream and chocolate molds; glass candy containers appeared in the familiar "cigar" shape of the "Los Angeles." All these are highly desirable to the collector, although the slow-moving, low-flying blimp (which in this jet age seems on a par with the kerosene lamp) was effective during World War II.

There's very little that can't find its way into an auction and a collector's heart: old tea-bag tags, poultry books, gas fixtures, old telephone cranks, railroad switch keys, pre-1935 railroad timetables. Some collectors do shy away from cloth antiques because they think they emit a strong aura of unsanitariness. "But," says the expert," if you've got the stomach to handle dirty, musty old pieces of cloth until you can get them washed or dry cleaned, you might be making one of the wisest antiques investments." Old fabrics, shawls, bed-spreads, horse blankets, bolt goods, linens, lead the list of sleepers in this kind of collecting. "If the old fabric you discover at an auction repels you, it shouldn't. As long as it's dry and not obviously wet, rotten, or wormy, it's just plain old dusty. Very few of the old time housekeepers packed things away

The new collector, who has been,
in recent times, a print collector,
might also look into African art, a
good and inexpensive field for
the beginner.

without cleaning them first, because they were costly and their owners nurtured them carefully, planning to pass them along."

If you see miniature furniture at an auction, don't assume it was made for children. In the old days, apprentices sometimes had to do small items from scrap wood before they were allowed to work with big pieces of good lumber. These miniatures were used as models to work from or even to take orders from. Children's toys were another matter, and they reach distinction faster than most other kinds of antiques because they're so perishable. Toys very often aren't saved, and because of that they're valued according to interest rather than age.

Real collecting can be an absorbing hobby; the collectibles don't have to be very expensive or difficult for an amateur to buy or look for. As the collection is filled in, the whole becomes more valuable—a good collection is worth more than the sum of its parts.

Contemporary limited editions

"They're producing limited editions in anything now to make them collectors' items," the auctioneer reports, "coins, bottles, animal sculptures, floral arrangements, medals, birds, mugs. I can forsee certain things that will make you money in ten years, but that doesn't mean just any old thing."

The business of supplying collectors with new objects in limited editions started gathering steam around 1960 and the throttle is wide open with no end of the lucrative trip in sight. The plate people are really cleaning up with their Limited Christmas

Editions. Some of the plates have been decorated by famous artists, like Wyeth and Rockwell and Dali, with designs that are popular and easily understood. Manufacturers promise to halt production of the plates forever at the end of the year, breaking the molds, but some of the limited editions aren't all that limited: Royal Copenhagen is said to have sold half a million of its 1971 plates in the U.S. alone. Resale prices seem to be shooting up, however. Wedgwood's 1971 Christmas plate was advertised seven months before Christmas for $30, with this appendage: "A small quantity of the 1970 Wedgwood plate still available at original price until August 31st. 1969 Wedgwood plate $125." In 1971 one Oregon auction gallery reported selling the 1969 plates for $200 each. For every collector who is enthusiastic about the plates, there's another who feels they're corny and saccharine. One auctioneer says it's fine to collect them for pleasure, but "despite the money that has been made, they're not very likely the proper field for long-range investments."

For the U.S. Bicentennial there is "a limited edition solid sterling massive art medal" of Washington crossing the Delaware, as well as "an unlimited edition in solid colonial pewter." Someday both of these will no doubt be bid in at auction higher than their original price. But whether they will be worth more than money left in the bank to accrue interest, is a gamble.

Collecting furnishings, curios, and works of art

Beyond our purview here are the connoisseurs' fields and the big money enterprises, like rare coins, stamps, museum pieces. However, there are available quite a number of undercollected and under-priced fine and interesting items. Here are a few you might consider:

Formal Sheraton furniture and furniture in the Duncan Phyfe style should be ideal for young collectors. They are fetching reasonable prices and in the near future will rise in value.

American trade cards: The cards and invoices of early merchants and professional men, one of the first forms of display advertising and used until after the Civil War, reveal not only a history of printing, but reflect the industries, occupations, arts, fashions, and social manners of early America. . . . Cards by unknown makers can be had from $1 to $3 and would make a decorative and lively collection. Also early shop signs in the shapes of animals, birds, clocks, boats.

Amusement park devices: penny arcade machines, Gypsy fortune-telling machines, carousel horses.

Ancient glass, particularly of the Roman period, first to fourth centuries A.D., has a good investment potential: Recent Parke-Bernet auction prices ranged from $30 to $150. . . . It is virtually impossible to fake ancient glass, and even a fairly inexperienced collector should soon be able to distinguish right from wrong. The most important factor is rarity of size, shape, or color, as there is a vast amount of ancient glass available.

Hair jewelry: unusual, inexpensive, plentiful. Hair woven, then braided, made into necklaces, brooches, etc. The originals were made of hair from a departed friend or lover, but after 1870 they were worn as a fad.

Bin labels of antique porcelain are little known and undercollected. The earliest were in tin enameled earthenware and date from the reign of James I. . . . By 1790 Josiah Wedgwood was making them in pearlware and Josiah Spode made bin labels in common earthenware as well as pearlware. Prices today run from $4 to $25.

British Prime Minister autographs: Although collectors have long been attracted by royalty . . . autographs of most British Prime Ministers, even major figures such as Disraeli and Gladstone, are plentiful and inexpensive.

Cane and umbrella handles: Ladies' and men's walking sticks, evening canes, parasols, and umbrellas all belong in this neglected field, (with their) multitude of knobs and handles, the diverse materials, the lavish decoration. Canes often had clandestine uses—hiding within them were swords, snuffboxes, and, during Prohibition, flasks. . . . Prices will rise once people realize the excellent craftsmanship and growing scarcity of these items. The beginner can certainly build up a handsome collection of eighteenth- and nineteenth-century examples for under $100.

Cattle and sheep paintings: For the past generation, such subject matter has been 'out.' Hundreds of really fine nineteenth-century European, English, and American paintings include these subjects. They are still priced below similar paintings without these animals and should prove to be buys for the future.

The new collector, who has been, in recent times, a print collector, might also look into African art, a good and inexpensive field for the beginner. An

experienced collector of African art says it's the
most adventurous of all pursuits, because since all
African artists are 'nameless' and without reputation,
the collector must evaluate the art all by himself.

Gruesomes

In olden times relics of saints were highly prized
by collectors who swore by their curative powers.
Today collectors are just as eager for the relics of
secular "saints," especially if their lives have been
scandalous or tragic. Napoleon relics head the
list. Besides personal items of clothing and furnishings he used, auctioned Napoleon relics include "a
small dried-up object genteely described as a
'mummified tendon,' taken from his body during
the post-mortem, not to mention 'a packet con-
taining specimens of the Emperor's hair (cranial,
facial, and pubic).'"

Humbug burrows everywhere. Modern relics, as
plentiful (and as authentic) as the several boatloads
of pieces of wood from the True Cross, have
brought riches to unscrupulous profiteers. One
credulous lady paid a great deal of money for
Nelson's glass eye, an object the Admiral never set
his own two eyes on. A highly imaginative Parisian
forger sold a letter written by Lazarus, after the
resurrection, in French.

The collecting bewares

1. Beware not to start if you don't want to get
hooked.

Collecting is a hard habit to break, and collectors
all too easily can become very greedy. You have to

guard against anything that becomes an obsession, especially to the ruination of the family exchequer.

2. Beware to consider how much you'll have to spend as you go along *before* choosing what to collect.

"Persons of moderate means are advised to dismiss hope of finding choice porcelain—it is better to look for English pottery." But whatever you collect, the chief value is the collection itself, because the intrinsic value is open to question. You can buy cheap for years, and if in the end you become overambitious or reckless and buy at much higher prices, you'll find your average of cost quite high.

3. Beware to give yourself a limit, in advance.

Decide on the number of pieces you're going to collect. Then instead of just adding more and more, take your worst piece and sell it and buy something better, keeping within your limited number. This is the best way to build a great collection.

4. Beware not to buy an item just to own it.

One auctioneer told me about people who thought they were collecting, "people who bought for years, who came to the auctions in streetcars with cash in their hands, to buy Limoges enamels worth hundreds of thousands of dollars. Then when their estate was auctioned, I found boxes of unpacked articles, my own tickets still on them. That kind of collecting may be a form of savings, but it's a disease too."

Others call it the magpie complex. "Buying without rhyme or reason, just to get their itching fingers on

The collecting nut is easy to recognize at an exhibition. He fondles an object in the manner peculiar to glass experts; having rubbed it against his cheek, touched it with his tongue and his nose, felt the pontil mark, and otherwise tested it, he issues his evaluation.

it; things piled in boxes, never used; every
shelf surface covered with bits and pieces, junk and
fine pieces cluttering up the house; to hoard just
for the sake of owning."

5. Beware of skirting all quality, or of quality in an
unreasonable amount.

The fellow who calls himself a collector because he
has a few buttons or some old comic books, is not
one really, because his so-called collection isn't
worth anything in monetary terms, but if he enjoys
going to auctions to look for additions to his
"collection," why not?

At the other extreme is the collector who is so
selective that he won't buy anything not made in
the northwest corner of Middlesex before 1843.
If he goes to enough auctions, some day he might
even come upon such an object, but meanwhile
he'll have to get his kicks from dreaming.

6. Beware not to let fashion dictate to you.

Auctions are often the most potent indication that
some new collecting mania has come into vogue,
but "if you follow only fashion you'll pay high
prices for inferior examples." Start your own fad. Be
adventurous, strike out on your own and do your
own discovering of what suits you.

7. Beware of assuming that all collectibles are
antiques (although all antiques are collectible).

If the word "pewter" is spelled out on the bottom
of a pitcher, for instance, it's not considered
"collectible" — it's too new. But if you like it, and
want it for your own use, and maybe to pass on to
your descendants, why not buy it?

Thousands of people have Sandwich glass in their cupboards, but it's late Sandwich glass, not the real Sandwich, and of no value at all. It's fine if it's there to enjoy; just don't expect it to bring money.

8. Beware of the reproduction game.

Reproductions are the bane of collectors. When reproductions of certain things (like milk glass, or scrimshaw) flood the market, they can ruin the value of the originals. "The moment you notice that your pieces are being imitated for the mass market at low prices, dispose of your collection as fast as you can. It will only get worse if you wait until reproductions have made your collection of little value and you can no longer display it with pride or realize anywhere near your original investment, or even pass it on as an heirloom."

If you're determined to start collecting autographs or books, which can reach to the skies in specialization and price but of which there are also many undercollected and inexpensive species, here are a few of the *BEWARES:*

There's no crash course for autograph collecting, but you can learn to recognize bona fide signatures. You can become familiar with the signatures of people in your field of interest—did they always sign their full name or their given name and initial? Is there evidence of erasures or retracings? In addition to the original signature, there are the proxy signatures (by secretaries or aides), and the machine signatures used by political figures who have thousands of documents to sign, and, of course, the forgery. Make certain, while you're learning to distinguish the genuine thing, that you're doing business with reliable and knowledgeable auctioneers or dealers.

If you want your autograph collection to have any long-term value, there's no point in buying things signed by people whose popularity is based on their name being in the news at the moment. Their signatures won't usually be worth much as soon as they fade off the TV screen.

If you decide to collect books, keep away from those that have long been the hunting ground for generations of collectors. Instead of starting with Shakespeare or early Reformation pamphlets, try home-life diaries, children's books by little-known authors, classics in economics or horticulture, or even seventeenth-century illustrated books.

The danger of fakes in books is not nearly as great as in works of art, but beware of books in bad condition. Avoid poor copies or imperfect ones, making sure they're complete, and wherever possible try to get the dust jacket, which often contains valuable material.

There are also plenty of nonaverage types. One auctioneer says his sales are often attended by members of the "syndicate" (formerly called the mob). Was he afraid? "Not at all. Some of them are my best customers."

7

THE WHEREFORES

In the early years of this century, a famous New York auctioneer said it was better business for him to let a woman get something at a very great bargain than a man, "for the woman will tell all her friends and they will all come the next day, while the man, getting something at a wonderfully low price, will tell of it, but won't tell where he got it."

Who buys at auction?

The Standard Oil millionaire, H. C. Folger, said the most exciting moment of his entire life came when he made a successful bid at an auction in 1899 which brought him his first original edition of Shakespeare, a Fourth Folio, for which he paid practically nothing ($107.50). His wife, who shared his passion for Shakespeare, said, "When a man and wife share such an interest it is the ultimate in felicity."

The super-rich may get all the attention, but a survey found that today's average auction-goer is less than forty-five years old, a member of the middle class, living in an American suburb, earning a comfortable income.

There are also plenty of nonaverage types. One auctioneer says his sales are often attended by members of the "syndicate" (formerly called the mob). Was he afraid? "Not at all. Some of them are my best customers. They start on the wrong side of the tracks, make money, buy fine books even if they don't know how to read. Gangsters are sometimes the best customers of auctions. The auction hides the names of people who buy. Even the government can't make them disclose the names."

Other than average types turn up in other places, too. An Alaskan who loved guns saw an auction advertised on Cape Cod; undaunted by January weather he flew from Alaska to the Cape to compete in person. Another Cape Cod auctioneer tells about a couple who were vacationing nearby early in the summer season. "Typical California types—he looked like a director, with bangs combed forward, dressed up very mod. She was very hotsy-totsy looking—high heeled sandals, tight pink pants, very blonde hair piled high. They looked around, asked, 'When's the auction, what kind of operation you got here? You give estimates? Yeh, well, tell me, how much for that pitcher? that chair? those bowls?' I told her what they were expected to go for. 'Listen, mister,' she said, 'couldn't you make your estimates a little lower?'" (They turned out to be good auction-goers, the auctioneer added, and showed up often during the summer.)

There are cynical auctioneers like the one out West who said, "Who goes to auctions? The collector; and the guy with larceny in his heart, the bargain hunters who love to steal something. Then there are people who can't afford retail price but love fine things, and auctions are the only way to get them. To be an auction buyer you must be very patient—you may have to work fourteen exhibitions before you find the piece you like. You could go to a decorator, but they're vultures."

Why

From the beginning of the fourteenth century, middle-class people in Europe bought various items at auction to make their homes more beautiful and more comfortable. Later, owning fine and beautiful objects became the tangible evidence of the possessor's new high ideals. In the eighteenth and nineteenth centuries, auction rooms were often the rendezvous places for high society and famous writers and artists. In America's days of settlement, people also started early to buy at auction, probably for more practical reasons than fashion or pride.

But there's no denying, says an oldtimer, that "an element of speculation predominates in the pursuit of an auction. If it weren't for the uncertainty there would be no thrill in the game. The lure is in the sport of adventure, not the mere acquisition." Maybe without being aware of it, auction buffs are subject to psychological factors like the gambling instinct, the excitement of bidding and unforseen endings, the desire to win. Auctions can also be an emotional thing for the buyer, "He hears his name over and over as he buys."

It's the same principle that keeps card-players going, to see what the next hand brings! Like horse-players, everybody hopes. People stay glued to their seats—on their faces it's written, not this item, but what comes next!

A New York auctioneer says, "Auctions are more popular today than ever—it's the upper class way of buying. It has panache, it's the in thing to do."

The young go to auctions to start a hobby or furnish a house. The middle-aged have a little more available money and find the auctions make less demand on their strength than store shopping. Auctions enrich the retirement years, when there's plenty of time, and they're an interesting outside activity.

A famous collector says that when he and his wife were young and poor, auctions were the best possible entertainment, and besides they were free. They are still described as a performance, like a theater piece. Spotlights are focused on the platform, on the auctioneer, and on each object as it's held up to be sold. There's a backstage crew of record-keepers and feeders; there are attendants who are supporting players and spear-carriers. When the curtain goes up, the master of ceremonies taps his gavel, and the audience stops talking and attends the stage. The first items up are "starters," giving the audience a chance to settle down. Then the action begins to build as the bidding mounts; the performance is in motion and each hammer blow becomes the climax of a drama. The excitement matches that of the racetrack or the gambling table, and the sport of getting something for less than its probable worth makes it even more appealing. "No matter how expert the auctioneer is," one of them admits, "he almost always has a blind spot. No one knows everything about everything, and sooner or later he's going to sell something for a great deal less than its true value."

There *must* be things purchased to advantage at auctions, because the same people keep coming back to them. "Go downtown," says a Boston auctioneer, "and compare prices and quality. It takes time and effort, but it's worth it—look at today's prices! For taste and style and value, even young people are frequenting auctions more and more, and they know quality; they've studied."

How

Observing a group of his contemporaries at the preview of an auction, Dr. Johnson described their reactions: "One looks with longing eyes and gloomy countenance on that which he despairs to gain from a rich bidder. . . . Another keeps his eye with care from settling too long on that which he most earnestly desires; and another, with more art than virtue, depreciates that which he values most, in hope to have it at an easy rate."

The auctioneer notes it if you show interest during the pre-sale viewing, so don't be too obvious or vocal. Obscure your real focus by showing an interest in everything. Auctioneers are pretty smart fellows, but they can't watch everybody all the time. If you know what you're doing, never let the auctioneer know what you want or that you have an interest in an item. You have to be leery if you're on your own — the auctioneer won't feel sorry for you or look out for the buyer who knows what he's doing.

After you find some auctioneers you have confidence in and like, leave word about your interests and they'll let you know when something like that is coming up in a sale. But if it's the kind of auction where there are no catalogues and the lot numbers are not taken in order, caveat emptor."

Go early to the auction and see everything possible. Dig in the boxes and open the drawers. And then keep track of everything you buy. It's important to

125

jot down each piece you buy, because you'd be surprised how easy it is to forget what you've bought and then forget to pick something up. It's just as important to note how much you're spending for each item, because that will keep you from buying more than you can pay for.

If you can divert your attention occasionally from the fast-paced proceedings, make a record of those things you're interested in and what they're selling for, grading them for condition and quality. It's all very helpful if you're going to become an inveterate auction-goer.

If you change your mind about something you've bought, or six months later you're tired of it, the auctioneer will reconsign it for you. Many buyers bring back and reconsign things. But at the time you're buying, the best advice to follow is if you have any doubt, leave it alone.

When

It is said that auctioneers prefer a one-day auction because prices are not usually so good the second day (which would make it better for us). There is a popular belief that bad weather usually means fewer buyers attending and again lower prices for us, but the consensus among the auctioneers seems to be that fairly bad weather works in their favor. As one auctioneer put it, "the weather is sometimes so terrible that everybody comes out thinking everybody else is going to stay home and he can steal bargains. Once I was ready to close the doors half an hour before the sale. Then a mob came." Every auctioneer has a story of the blizzard or the flood they thought would keep anyone from showing up, and then the crowds that came out because they thought no one else would.

Sometimes it's wise to stay at an auction till the very last minute. When a sale has lagged late into the afternoon or evening, the audience has thinned out and gotten a bit drowsy, the auctioneer grown tired, there are often marvelous things to get at low, low bids.

Sometimes it's wise to stay at an auction till the very last minute. When a sale has lagged late into the afternoon or evening, the audience has thinned out and gotten a bit drowsy, the auctioneer grown tired, there are often marvelous things to get at low low bids.

Sources of merchandise

All the stories that must lie behind the multitude of items put on the auction block defy the imagination. One of England's very early auctions consisted of goods belonging to a returning English governor of India, who was none other than Eli Yale—born in Boston and taken back to England when he was ten.

Sometimes auctions have their beginnings in disaster. It took the French Revolution to put on the block most of the furnishings and treasures of Versailles. One of the earliest held auctions in America offered the belongings of a poor fellow by the name of Sir Danvers Osborne, who had been appointed a governor of New York. He arrived in 1753 with great hopes for his career and with a household of furniture. He hanged himself five days after his arrival, "on account of private griefs and threatened public troubles," (which sounds like nothing so much as threatened disclosure of private scandal).

Today auctions are usually held to settle estates, to liquidate bankrupt firms, or to collect delinquent taxes or unpaid customs or storage fees of unclaimed goods.

Some auctions are just signs of the times. When the Paramount Theater building in New York was

128

scheduled for demolition, the contents of still another luxury palace of the movies' heyday ended up in the auction houses. (There were paintings and marble statues and bronzes and fine furniture and china and pianos and chandeliers and endless bric-a-brac).

Estates are sold for various reasons: the old owner dies; the family loses its money; there's a divorce or separation; or the last members of a dwindling family die out. Estate-owners may simply want to move into small apartments. Sometimes they have no heirs and want the satisfaction of seeing where their effects go, knowing what they're valued at. "They have little stories about each piece," says a country auctioneer, "and I like to have them at the auction." A city auctioneer says, "If they own the collection, we advise them not to come to the sale, because they value everything differently."

The reasons for selling vary from the auction advertised as "a complete household, moved here from England by a career serviceman who is now being transferred again," to contemporary art collectors who say: "We never could fit that 17-foot painting into the living room and we want to convert some of the collection into cash"; or "I want to rearrange things in the house, bring in a lot of young people. We've decided to let these few things go out into the world, because they're history, darling, and I'm not involved with history."

Sometimes goods come to the auction block by way of titillating drama. In the mid-1950s there was an auction in Chicago of the jewels of Countess di Frazzo, who had been found dead in her Santa Fe train compartment by the actor Clifton Webb. The Countess, found clad in a black sequin evening gown and mink coat, a $100,000 diamond necklace, and a 10-karat diamond ring, was "an internationally known movie and night-club social figure who mixed with nobility and the underworld."

The background was nothing if not dramatic a few years ago when a New York auctioneer was engaged by a bank to sell the estate of Winifred Bird. This lady, after willing her worldly goods to her doctor and her boyfriend, had then been dispatched by them with slow poison, in Paris. Back at the Long Island estate garage, several antique cars, left untouched for more than twenty years since her husband's death, were auctioned off. The piece de resistance of a separate lot was a diamond necklace that went for over six figures. All in all it was a goodly estate, but the murderers' interest was moot, as last heard of they were still languishing in prison.

Auctions usually have more family-type back-grounds. Many things are sold two and three times, a New England house points out. "For example, an Oriental rug I sold to a family five years ago for $600 has now been sent back to me to sell for them. They're moving away and the rug won't fit their new house. They'll make a profit on it after having enjoyed and used it for five years. Buy good things and you won't lose."

Even when very fine items disappear into museums they surface again on rare occasions. Museums do sell their surplus at auction. They may be over-crowded or have duplicates, or too many pieces that were inexpensive and easy to get when they began but whose space they now need for more important items. Or the museum might have changed its ideas and image over the years. Sometimes they don't want it known when they're getting rid of things, so they call in auctioneers and ask them to work them into some future sales.

"During the Great Depression of the 1930s there were auctions at furniture stores, and the rich drove up in the middle of the night to unload," remembers an oldtimer. There were many auctions then on behalf of creditors. They were almost a barometer of business conditions, for there are fewer such auctions in good times, while the number sharply increases in bad times.

In good times auction houses may even resort to espionage to find likely sources of goods, particularly merchandise like antiques, which are not reproducible and are limited in amount. World-renowned auction houses watch obituary columns for leads; they have spies on the lookout for whoever might be thinking of getting rid of his old armor or any other treasures. Any trick or promise is fair. An important New England auctioneer was once vying with Christie's and Parke-Bernet for a big estate of important Oriental rugs, and he got it by promising the old owner a picture of each rug and a leatherbound copy of the catalogue.

Dealers can be sellers at auction as well as buyers. "When the auctioneer says 'items from several other New England collectors,' it could mean several other dealers," says one of them. "Half the dealers need money and half of them are getting rid of some of their stuff."

The low men on the totem pole are those who make a living by cleaning out others' attics and cellars for nothing, and then bringing any saleable items to the auctioneer.

Legalities

Some states (and eventually it should be all) license auctioneers. State laws protect the public from misrepresentation by the auctioneer and protect auctioneers from the abuses sometimes visited on them by callous bidders and conniving dealers.

The auctioneer walks a tightrope between the consignor and the bidder; he is the agent of the owner until he accepts the buyer's bid, and then he becomes the buyer's agent, seeing that the buyer receives his goods according to the condition of the sale.

The auctioneer is bound to accept any legitimate bid by a responsible person, and as soon as that hammer comes down, the contract is made, obliging the buyer to buy and the seller to sell. But until the final fall of the hammer, the auctioneer can withdraw an item from sale, *unless* it has been advertised to be sold "without reserve." A bidder may also withdraw his bid any time before the gavel's final rap.

If a dispute develops, the property can be put up for sale again at the last undisputed price, or the auctioneer can withdraw it to present it at another time. Conflict is solved at Parke-Bernet by an old rule which says that the bidder nearest the auctioneer wins. Years ago a jeweler bid at that house for the famous Idol's Eye diamond; his bid was simultaneous and identical with that of a competitor, but because of the geography of his seat, he was awarded the prize.

Each lot is bought at the buyer's risk and removed at the buyer's expense. The terms of the sale are

132

specifically stated in the catalogue, and it is usually specified that everything is sold as is. "No statement, orally or in the catalogue, is a warranty."

If goods are not paid for, they can be resold, and the difference between that price and the first one has to be paid by the first buyer (if and when he's ever found).

In states where auctioneers are not yet licensed, there are Auctioneers' Associations pledged to a code of ethics drawn up by the National Auctioneers' Association. The auctioneer should be helpful, examine each piece before the sale and tell you whether it's old or a reproduction, determine its authenticity, and answer your questions. We might be leery of all these requirements, but reputable auctioneers say they have a reputation to defend and so wouldn't knowingly misinform. "We wouldn't stay in business long if we made a practice of selling soapstone and calling it jade."

There is even a form of unwritten guarantee, despite the disclaimers in the conditions of sale. Top houses allow a twenty-one day period during which items can be returned, if they are proved to be grossly different from the catalogue description. For nonprofessional buyers in New York, state law extends that period to one year, and it gives legal recourse to buyers "whenever the catalogue or bill of sale describes a work of art as being by a named author or of a named period, culture, source, or origin."

"Must have cost her a couple of hundred dollars to come down and get that Indian," the auctioneer marveled.

8

THE SPECIES AUCTIONEM

One day a little old lady about eighty drove up
to an auction on Cape Cod in a Yellow Taxi, all the
way from Boston ($80 on the meter). She had the
cab wait for her all afternoon, and then took it back
to Boston, sitting there in the back of the taxi
beside a cigar store wooden Indian she had bought
at the auction.

"Must have cost her a couple of hundred dollars to
come down and get that Indian," the auctioneer
marveled.

You are probably familiar only with a few kinds of
auctions — those that offer art objects, furnishings,
rare coins or stamps or books, cigar store Indians —
but also sold at auction are crops, used cars,
real estate, beef on the hoof, the stock of bankrupt
businesses, fresh fish, warehouse unclaimeds,
government surplus, and much more.

Occasionally these days, what's known as a
Hollywood Auction is held to sell out the trappings
of a studio, like an Ingrid Bergman suit of armor
from *Joan of Arc*, Herb Alpert's yellow vinyl
blazer, or the boat from *Showboat*. They're very
popular auctions (which can be participated in by
mail by anyone who doesn't live in the environs
of the studios), especially with nostalgia addicts
who treasure items used by the Silver Screen's
great and near-great.

Large cities have *Post Office Auctions* of damaged goods or nondeliverable packages. The merchandise can include watches, books, tools, sterling silver, crystal, paintings, furniture, toys, clothing, TV sets, radios—you name it. Small objects like lighters and raincoats and pen knives are sold in lots of 20 to 500; larger things are sold individually.

Public auctions take place once or twice a year at police departments, where anything can turn up in the lost and found, according to the variety of interests and degree of absent-mindedness of the public. Almost every police station has at least an auction of unclaimed or recovered stolen bicycles.

At port cities there are periodic *Customs House Auctions,* where the merchandise sold includes (1) unclaimed goods, perhaps lacking identifying labels, which have been held for a year; (2) "abandoned" merchandise, purposely left by the addressee because it wasn't satisfactory and by abandoning it he saved paying duty; (3) objects confiscated from sailors which they were apparently trying to smuggle in. The first two categories are usually large lots, by the gross or truckful; the third category can yield some very interesting small items.

Charity Auctions range from the neighborhood sale sponsored by the St. John's Ladies Guild "featuring new items, ideal for gift-giving, used and old articles," to the ultra chic affair, like the one held in Denver where a balloon ascension with astronaut Wally Schirra or a week at a famous beauty spa were on the block. Everything falls under the hammer for a good cause. Knowledgeable auction-goers like church auctions and fund-raising sales in small towns; because they're run by amateurs, one can often uncover a good find. 136

Charity auctions are especially popular in summer colonies during the season, and are often highlighted by items donated by famous residents. Workers for noble causes have found they raise funds painlessly by soliciting antiques that have lost their appeal for the present owner. Since summer houses are often the last resting place for objects people have changed their minds about, and since local dealers also donate items to these auctions, there's no telling what might turn up.

Most fund-raising art auctions are run by professionals whose business is just such events. But there are occasional charity auctions (usually newsworthy) where professional auctioneers donate their time for charitable purposes, like the Kennedy fund-raising auction at the Institute of Contemporary Art.

Wine Auctions, which are gaining popularity and notoriety (the successful bidder for a $5000 bottle having appeared on television), have two advantages: You can often buy wine cheaper than in the stores, and you can buy rarities you won't see anywhere else. They also have disadvantages: You have to buy in relatively large quantities, you run the risk of being carried away and paying too much.

To develop confidence in your own palate experiment with various wines from wine merchants before venturing into the very tricky wine auction. Check up on the reputation of the seller and be sure you can trust his descriptions, for an inevitable hazard of buying the rarer and older wines is the gamble you take on their condition and quality.

Wanna buy a used car? How about this one that was only used by a suicide club for the carbon monoxide? Well that kind of selling is old hat. Used cars are sold individually by auction now to retail buyers, and the ordinary car buyer is finding that such sales can mean a bargain for him. America's largest auto auctioneer tells his franchisees all over the country to depend on small profit and large volume, and it apparently works, because the comparable prices indicate a considerable saving over lot sticker prices, even after allowing for the usual haggling.

A good used car auctioneer is the one who checks every car out thoroughly (one runs it through an electronic diagnostic center) and posts the findings on the windshield. One company also permits the return of any of their auctioned cars for any reason whatsoever, assuming it is in the same physical condition as when sold, within seven days for a refund of 90 percent (which sometimes is cheaper than renting a car for the week).

The hoopla is wild at used car auctions—there's a carnival atmosphere, sometimes the excitement of a carny pitchman, and as always there's the danger of overexuberance that might send the bidding beyond reason. Still, there's a certain credibility at a good used car auction that many of the regular used-car lots have been forfeiting lately.

There's another kind of used car auction held periodically where you can buy the likes of a 1930 Ford Model A popcorn wagon or a 1925 Kissel speedster or a 1934 Lagonda sports tourer. Buyers come from all over this country and from Europe and South America to these auctions, which are very posh affairs. It's the place to go even if you're just interested in looking at a 1909 International Harvester car which not only carried passengers but could be converted to serve as a truck. Apparently these auctions have buyer bargains and the same pressures as any other auction—the day before one, I heard the auctioneer on the phone, "Cross it off! I don't know. The wife got nervous and sold the car to a private offer. The car's withdrawn, that's all. She's perfectly willing to pay a penalty."

There seem to be two kinds of *Rug Auctions,* one of which provokes unkind words from critical auctioneers. They have nothing against antique rug auctions (Oriental, Persian, French, etc.), which are comparable to auctions for any other kind of fine antiques. At a very important auction of some well-known rug collection, buyers will come to compete from all over the country and from several continents (some in private planes).

The more common auctions of new or used modern Oriental rugs are what draw attacks from professionals. Usually the rug merchants themselves run these auctions and usually they own the rugs. A notable auctioneer says, "Check on rug sales, analyze the economy of it, compare it to retail selling. It takes very judicious buying to get a bargain."

Door prizes every hour are often offered at these auctions, and some advertise a "One year warranty which permits the buyer to exchange the rug for any other of comparable value."

An auctioneer who travels all over America and England selling Persian rugs is described as smooth as cream, selling along with his Bokharas and Sarouks, the joys of ownership: "Madame if I had to go to the bank and borrow money, I'd invest in this one," or "You couldn't even buy an oilcloth this size for that amount," or "The Mona Lisa of Rugdom . . . what? the fringe is off the bottom? Madame, nothing in this world is perfect, except what God himself has made . . . soft like a piece of chamois skin . . . it hung on the wall of a deposed king, I'm not allowed to tell you who he was, his name begins with F and ends with K, SOLD! You'll have a lovely home, dear, you've made two wonderful buys."

One auctioneer says, "Rug auctions? That's a form of buying retail. The dealer sells at auctions because he can sell his stock in one night or two— it's a fast form of sale. Otherwise, it could take a year or so. Another told me, "The first rug goes at a very good price, and they cry bitterly over it. It gets things going. Usually the rugs sell pretty close to retail price at the auction. But if you go in and offer in advance you can buy a rug for as much as 35 percent under the market price." All of which is not to say that they aren't good rugs. Most of them are (just watch if they call them "domestic Oriental," which means they are NOT handmade) and you can get good buys *if* you are judicious— especially, it would seem, if you buy the first one put up.

Our final example of miscellaneous auctions may top them all: *Birthright Auctions,* sometimes known as the Ghoul Pool, which is selling your inheritance before the legator who bequeathed it has gone to his final reward.

The scene of this quiet, steady birthright selling looks like something out of Charles Dickens and sounds like Charles Addams. The inheritance is described in legal euphemism as a "reversion," and 140

Following the country auctions is as hard to stop as "peanut-eating." Country auctions are held all over the land, with folksy auctioneers selling millions of dollars worth of used goods, antiques and someday-to-be-antiques.

the reversioner can sell his uncle's trust fund or his wife's life insurance policy or his grandmother's estate without any of them knowing about it, while grandma and the others get an "alien heir" who is a total stranger. The name and condition of health of the property owner are kept carefully hidden until after the sale is completed.

The auction, which takes place in London, may go something like this: "For sale by private treaty the life interest of a lady, age 59, in one-third of the income from a trust fund, which at present produces an income of $500,000 per annum. The trust is subject to the laws of the State of California, USA. Can I tempt your bid, sir, or you sir, over there?"

Maybe a trust fund of blue chip stocks and bonds, currently worth more than three times its sale price, reverts to a successful bidder — but not until the seller's 65-year old mother dies. An expert says the buyer shouldn't hold his breath. The actuarial tables give the woman 15½ years more, but one company that invests in reversions says they have held a few listings as long as 40 years. They also say they never have had any contact with the life tenants for whom, purely as a matter of investment, they are waiting on to die. But it's not as bad as it sounds — in the old days bounders used to finance their escapades and gambling debts by selling their inheritances; today it usually stems from more mundane needs, like buying a house or sending a child to college.

Country and Podunk auctions

Following the country auctions is as hard to stop as "peanut-eating." Country auctions are held all over the land, with folksy auctioneers selling millions of dollars worth of used goods, antiques and someday-to-be-antiques. It's a toss-up whether summer or fall is the best season, but when the weather turns cold the auctions thin out considerably or go indoors till spring. The names are often picturesque like "Egypt Hill Auction and Farmers Market," or "Treasure and Trash." One pocket in America's farflung country auction activity is in the central eastern states around New Jersey, Pennsylvania, Maryland, and Virginia, where they have quaint names like Intercourse, Pa., which is near Bird-in-hand and Paradise. The Intercourse Flea Market, has auctions too, and one fellow who's been auctioneering there for years is fond of saying he's never found a flea yet.

A New England "podunk" auctioneer describes his audiences to me as "one-third auction hounds who come all the time. Sometimes they're just seat-warmers, but they all buy from time to time. Another third comes out of curiosity, looking for entertainment—it's their first time or they saw a gas heater advertised. The other third are dealers, the basis of all auctions. If I have a value, they'll bid on it."

A typical podunk auction is held in a rented hall, attended by locals, with some teenagers sprinkled around and many younger children. Everybody will be happily eating. ("The auction opens when the coffee's ready," says a habitué). At first the 200 chairs may hold 100 people and then by 7:20 they're suddenly full. Men with canvas carpenter's aprons (2-pocket model holding money instead of nails) are the runners who deliver the goods and pick up the cash at once from the winning bidder. Merchandise boxes on chairs indicate some have already bought things before the auction.

On the tables are the goods that will be auctioned—
much new stuff (lamps, candy dishes) some small
appliances (coffee pot, iron), painted milk cans,
boxes of outdated books, the inevitable print of
"The Death of Mr. Lincoln"; on the floor is furniture
from the 1930s (a kitchen set, half-moon end tables,
a vanity chair).

People come to socialize—you can't hear or see for
the yakking and the standing in the aisles, their
backs to the auctioneer, talking talking talking.
The auction starts early so they can bring the kids
(no babysitter problems). They call back and forth,
"Hey, mac, where were you Sunday?" or "How you
buying tonight?" The auctioneer makes an
announcement about a colleague who "grabbed
one of those old lamps that need rewiring; the
microphone is a conductor, see, it's not grounded.
That lamp shorted. Almost electrocuted him. They
gave him mouth to mouth and he's in the hospital.
Don't know if there's brain damage."

Everybody's talking and standing in the aisles
chattering while the auctioneer is working. You
can hardly hear him, but it doesn't seem to bother
him. ("Three and a half now. All this stuff is brand
new, came out of a house, believe it or not, came
out of a house just like you see it, do I hear 3.75?")

Two women at nearby tables are keeping records;
there are three runners, and three little kids are
handing things up to the auctioneer. He holds up a
half-gallon jar of nails, "This here's a jar full of
coat hangers," the auctioneer shouts over the noise.
He points to a wooden clothes wringer, "There's an
antique for you. Dated July 1867." (They all do it—
read the date of patent and think it's the date of

144

manufacture, as if everybody must have dated their clothes wringers). The auctioneer pats it, "You got some wet money?"

Country auctions are often held outdoors in the yard of the house the merchandise comes from. People bring their own chairs, or stand. Two very large ladies appropriate an old-time school bench with a dangling auctioneer's numbered tag, remove the seat to the audience area, and occupy it (or as much of it as they can), while a hopeful bidder hovers around hoping it will be put up on the block.

Kids are singing, people are talking, the auctioneer is apparently unperturbed and determinedly cheerful. He can't always hear the bids, so the bidder's neighbors whistle and point to the timid bidder, shouting out "Here! Fellow over here!"

A couple of known dealers who showed up earlier are nowhere to be seen — they probably left a bid for anything they were interested in. The auctioneer's wife runs the refreshment stand selling homemade cakes, sandwiches, and drinks. Two young girls hand items to the auctioneer and collect cash on the spot from bidders. A few kids scream and are hushed by their parents, some of whom have beards and long hair and bare feet.

The auctioneer holds up an old contraption and asks for an opening bid, keeps asking, no one responds. He's having a hard time getting an opening bid and that contraption looks interesting, so what the heck, I half-wave $1. At that moment he takes a sudden bid, louder and stronger than mine, for $10, then quickly another for $15. I go to get coffee. "There were good pocketbooks in the

audience," he tells me later, "Never let 'em stop
to breathe."

"You got to be nice to your people," says an
auctioneer from up country, "otherwise you never
have no crowd. But sometimes you get irritated.
This here fella, everything we put up, he bid a
quarter. Everything was a quarter. We got a box
next to the stand where we throw anything broken
or chipped, so my son, he kicked it around some
for a while, then he handed it to me, and that
fella, there he was again, again a quarter. He got it."

"Or you get people that will battle over a dollar
item," he continues. "Somebody will pay double
what something's worth, just so Mr. Soandso won't
get it. I was selling a vase, wasn't worth more'n
$25. I wanted to stop—I don't like to see something
go for a lot more than it's worth, because they're
going to wake up when they get home, and then
I've lost a customer. 'Ladies, ladies!' I told them
when they got to $75—'Don't you dare stop!'
they said. That thing, would you believe it, went
for $100!"

A smoother type who runs slightly more sophisti-
cated auctions also says it: "These people have to
be your friends, too. People will go away angry
if they get insulted or are given the shaft—I mean
driven into a corner for something they don't want.
Big city audiences are constantly changing, but
small town auctions get the same people over and
over.

"I had a big copper anchor from Holland—they
used to be fastened to the top of the anchor
chain so you could tell where the bow is—made
by the same company who made the original ones

a hundred years ago. They sell for $99 at the surplus store. I told the audience this when I put it up. The bidding started at $50, a young couple down front. Some fellow in the back was competing against them, and they all got carried away. The bidding reached $140. Everybody was tittering at such suckers. I thought, I'm not going to let them be embarrassed, so I said to the man in the back, 'I'm going to sell this to this young couple for $65, and next week I'll have one here for you at the same price.'

"Everybody in the audience thought I was a great guy; I now had two loyal customers, and I was happy because I made $20 apiece on the anchors."

Maybe these fellows exaggerate the figures up or down, but there's no doubt that they know how to get along with the characters who come to their auctions. One auctioneer said he sometimes gets a wiseacre dropping in at the auction "after the bar closes. It's his first time at an auction, he's just out for a good time. For something worth $25, he'll bawl 'ten cents!' The drunks are the most obnoxious characters we get, but I make friends of most of them. Some nights I invite them to come up front. Either they disappear out the door or they come up, and then I know they're extroverts. 'Want to try to auction something?' I'll say, and they do. Everybody laughs and he has a good time and that's the end of it."

A rural auctioneer says "general merchandise" is the hardest kind of auction to run. "It doesn't take an auctioneer to sell a good piece—it sells itself. I sell one good item in 3 minutes for $50, but it takes 10 or 15 minutes to get $50 for 'general merchandise'" (his euphemism for junk).

Among the objects a TV auction in the east put on the block: ten hours of flight instruction "to a qualified person"; a descented skunk, among other more conventional animals; 10,000 pieces of bubble gum; a ride on a circus elephant; enough hamburgers to feed a family of four for one year; 1000 chicken wings; 400 pounds of birdseed; all kinds of parties; a trip to the Caribbean on the Queen Elizabeth II; a 15-foot blue spruce; and a hawk.

Country auctioneers are aware of their supposed hick ignorance, and they use the image to good advantage. In addition to their local merchandise, they have city pickers and runners visiting them regularly with stock from the metropolis, which city people sometimes come and bid on and take back with them.

Cosmopolitan auctioneers admit, "You can find real good buys anywhere at country auctions, although you won't find a $25,000 painting for $8. And some things bring more than retail price. The more primitive the auction, the smarter you better be as a buyer. Those farm auctions, run by an auctioneer who wears suspenders and has a straw in his mouth and a twangy spiel . . ."

There might be plenty of ramshackle monstrosities bought for a few dollars, to be touched up and sold for a lot of money in some far away shop, but there also might be an odd looking chair or a lovely old bowl to be kept and prized.

Commercial auctions

Commercial auctions are usually better left to professional businessmen, but occasionally there will be an auction on something like a moribund hotel or theater, or a defunct gift shop or nursery landscaping stock. The merchandise from most such businesses, which are retiring from the lists for one reason or another (bankruptcy, liquidation, etc.), is auctioned in quite large lots and is often not up-to-date goods. However, if you want to chance it, just be sure you know current market value and the condition of whatever you bid on. At one stationery store auction someone watching said, "I

can't figure it out. They're bidding over the retail
prices printed on the boxes. Can't they read?''
When an old German restaurant was auctioned off
in Chicago, the newspapers noted that a wardrobe
rack brought exactly four times the price it could
have been bought for new in most any store.

Real estate

The reasons people sell a house or a building or
land at auction are familiar: the owner is in financial
difficulties, there's been a death in the family,
bankruptcy, foreclosure (not very common these
days, as banks try to help), the non-payment of
taxes, divorce settlement, or perhaps something
as simple as the owner wanting to move to Florida
and not hang around and wait to sell his property.

Buying real estate at auction, says a prominent
specialist in the field, is like buying at any auction —
supply and demand. He urges bidders to ask questions, ''as many as necessary and never mind how
silly sounding.'' Real estate auctions don't take
hours and days to conduct, the way estates do —
the bidding procedure is over in fifteen minutes or
so. But it's not all that cut and dried; a lot goes on
beforehand and a lot afterwards. ''You can't just
sell a piece of property bang bang bang, but usually
subject to court conditions. It's quite complicated,
and therefore the bidder should have an attorney.
He has to bring papers, make transfer arrangements,
all that sort of thing.''

''You should talk to the auctioneer beforehand,
call him up, or go in and see him. He's always willing. But you're going to have to hire an attorney for
the final transaction anyway, why not have him

represent you at the auction and advise you on
the property before?"

You have to understand completely what you're
buying. First, as a buyer, you have to know what
you can do with the property. Do you want to
live there? Can you live there, legally? Can you get
the financing that will allow you to do what you
want with the property? Can you afford it? And
every real estate auctioneer says the same thing
every other auctioneer says—predetermine exactly
how much you want to bid and don't go over it.

You may see "building lots" advertised for auction,
but the question is, is it a *buildable* lot. There
are matters of sewers, water supplies, technical
digging conditions; if it's not approved by the town,
it's not a buildable lot. And of course to bid on
land that you've never seen is sheer folly.

"Legal notices," says the auctioneer, "don't elicit
a great deal of public interest, so they're a good
place to find property being auctioned that you
might be interested in."

Auctions on the small silver screen

A new phenomenon abroad in the land—one that's
bound to increase with our days—is the television
auction by (and raising funds for) almost every
major educational network from coast to coast
and in between. Los Angeles' third annual TV
auction, for instance, comprised of over 4000 items,
raised $250,000 on $400,000 worth of donated
merchandise. They made money and bidders got
bargains. Boston's sixth annual TV auction raised
$450,000 ($75,000 over their previous year) with
105,000 recorded bids.

Businesses and individuals by the thousands donate merchandise for altruistic and advertising reasons — in California "if your donation exceeds $25 in retail value your name will be mentioned prior to the auctioning and again upon purchase."

What can you buy on TV auctions? A lot more than you can buy anywhere else in the world: cars; an autographed Arnold Palmer golf glove; a charter cruise on a 65-foot ketch for five days complete with captain and cook; a 42-week secretarial course; 500 cat houses; a ten-foot boa constrictor and a fifteen-foot sandwich.

Among the objects a TV auction in the east put on the block: ten hours of flight instruction "to a qualified person"; a descented skunk, among other more conventional animals; 10,000 pieces of bubble gum; a ride on a circus elephant; enough hamburgers to feed a family of four for one year; 1000 chicken wings; 400 pounds of birdseed; all kinds of parties; a trip to the Caribbean on the Queen Elizabeth II; a 15-foot blue spruce; and a hawk. The authorities appeared suddenly in the case of that last item, informing the successful bidder that the hawk was classed as an endangered species and it was illegal to buy one at auction or to own one without a license — IF it had flown into the state under its own power. However, if the hawk had been flown in by plane, the endangered species classification didn't apply.

In Los Angeles a check for ten cents signed by Jack Benny, in the 1950s, and made out to Dean Martin and Jerry Lewis (his part of a restaurant tip) was auctioned, as was a private lunch with Martha Mitchell. One lady in San Francisco thought she was the winning bidder for a ticket on the Italian

Greyhound Line when she had actually bought a gift certificate for stud service of an Italian greyhound dog.

Behind the cameras, these sorts of things are called 'panic items, i.e. those which engender tremendous enthusiasm, like dinner with David Susskind or team-signed hockey sticks. The regular best sellers are more prosaic: autos, TVs and radios, hardware, jewelry, foods, services, entertainment, and financial items, like savings accounts and $2 bills.

Annual TV auctions started in San Francisco in 1956 and have since spread all over the country. The educational stations start working on the next auction as soon as one is finished, their all-volunteer force numbering up to 4500 people. During the auction (usually one whole week) there are several tables of merchandise going at all times, the first being presented on camera while volunteers manning the phones are taking bids for the items on the other tables. The amounts bid are posted on big boards, and there's no time lag—you have to bid fast or you won't get it, except on big items, which are shown twice and may take several hours to sell.

"Stick by your phones so we can confirm the high bids," they tell listeners, "If you are high bidder the auctioneer will announce your name." They time items by certain parts of the day, those aimed at the housewife in the afternoon, cars at night when fathers are home, kids' things early. "There are certain obvious prohibitions," one station says. Maybe they were thinking of the service of a stud horse, which, as a result of innumerable calls (they refused to elaborate) they said "we'll never do that again!"

A bidder at a Wisconsin TV auction advises that it's best if you can wait to see what bids are in; hang on the phone so you can raise if you want to.

Most of the art and antiques auctioned off are handled differently from other goods. Usually they're put on exhibition for a week before the auction, and the bidding starts then, "silently." You write your name and bid on the page of a book for that specific work of art—if somebody raises you, you can go back and raise your bid. There is further bidding sometimes on the TV screen, but it's certainly better to go and see the art first, beforehand. One high bidder for a painting refused on sight to take it because there was "too much color." His TV set was black and white.

The volunteer auctioneers are mostly guest celebrities —baseball players, movie directors' wives, a governor or senator and various politicians, show biz personalities, bearded professors and other academic personnel. In the middle-west experts in the area from art and archaeology museums review everything on pertinent tables before the auction opens. In California one of the volunteer auctioneers got carried away and sold the station's logo-type for about half what it cost them to replace it. (That may have been the same auctioneer who sold two male and two female chinchillas off in pairs—same-sex pairs).

European auctions

England

For about two hundred years, until the advent of the U.S. contender, London's most famous auction houses have been cock of the walk in the

Heated arguments often interrupt the rapid bidding.

English-speaking world. Since their founding in the 18th century, Sotheby's and Christie's have been among the world's largest clearinghouses of art objects of all kinds, symbols of luxury. In 1795, Christie's sold the jewels of Madame la Comtesse du Barry after she was put to death for smuggling them out of revolutionary France to the haven of Mr. Christie's auction rooms. "Valuable Jewels, of most singular Excellence, Beauty, and Perfection," they were described, and for their so-called "theft from the State" France beheaded la Comtesse.

Today the British auction goods very similar to those auctioned in America, and Sotheby's has merged with the American champion, Parke-Bernet. Christie's and Sotheby's are often consigned goods in the United States, ship them to London for auction, and may very well ship them back to the U.S. for an American buyer. (Whatever you deduce from that pricewise, fit this one in: French dealers are said to be cleaning out the British auction houses, buying in England and selling at considerable profit in France.)

The cognoscenti agree that American auctions are more exciting than the British. An English auction can be dreary at its worst, although at its best the auctioneer does like to present a dramatic production. He just does it in a more leisurely fashion than his American counterpart. In London's better auction houses (Sotheby's and Christie's are only two of several) auctioneers just announce the price actually bid, without suggesting an increment. They use British understatement that we call the soft-sell, rarely wrapping anything in the enticing hyperbole that points out the object's virtues. This is generally attributed to the audiences, the British being mostly dealers and skilled collectors who "make the sale almost anti-climactic." In America the auction itself is the climax, as private buyers predominate.

A chronicler of English auctions says they are geared to "the trade," the middlemen. He described London salesrooms as "a jumble of dusty merchandise which passes for an exhibition," thus the tyro is assumed incapable of judging anything for himself and needs advice from an expert, i.e. dealer. "The American exhibition has a comparatively well-scrubbed look with a warts-and-all approach to the catalogue, listing defects clearly, instilling a customer's confidence in his own judgment. The British catalogue pays little attention to all but the large obvious flaws," which means the cautious customer looks to the dealer for advice.

However, England's Misrepresentation Act doesn't allow the auctioneer to put the responsibility on the buyer, and provides remedy for anyone who has been misled by a false description. Also, there are no Federal, state or city taxes on merchandise purchased at auction in England as there are in America.

Auctioneers who import English antiques for their American sales rooms say that for the traveler to buy anything while he's abroad too big to carry home with him is "too complicated. The objects have to be set up for a shipper (after you find one), crated and taken through customs. Then they have a lot of red tape to go through at this end. It's not worth it. All these things we buy are sent containerized, taken care of in lots by well-organized warehouses."

Sotheby's has opened a special branch in the fashionable Belgravia section of London that deals exclusively with 19th and early 20th century art and artifacts (said to be the most significant trend developing in the 1970s — "Where 18th century was the catchword of the '60s, 19th century is the motto of the '70s.")

France

The national pawn shop of France, the Monts de Piete (official title, Credits Municipaux), handles auction sales almost every day in Paris, although there are certain days for selling certain things. Every weekday when the bells of the church next door strike two p.m., the doors open for the auction sales of unredeemed merchandise like cameras, sewing machines, fur coats, carpets, jewelry, clothes. Most things go very cheaply, the audience being mainly French housewives and flea market and junk shop dealers whose pride and purse prevent them from overpaying. The commissionaire says "bon courage" when he gives you a catalogue.

The biggest mixed sales are held in France's largest auction house, the Hotel Drouot, where the 18 salesrooms are called *salles de ventes* and where the properties of such notables as Chopin, Mistinguett and "Camille" have been sold. The good sales are judged by the size and impatience of the crowd waiting to get in when lunch hour is over, and by their mad rush to get the front seats.

Heated arguments often interrupt the rapid bidding, but most of what is bought and sold at auction in Paris moves through these rooms: treasures once hoarded by collectors, estates whose owners are no more, household goods seized by creditors, smuggled goods confiscated by Customs. Dealers from the flea market and the junk shops come here, but so do the antiquaries, the collectors, and just about everybody else who wants to buy something at auction.

Renoir used to tell the story of how in 1872 he and his painter friends held an auction of their works at the Hotel Drouot in order to raise some badly needed money. It caused a riot, which did them a lot of good. A detractor who went around ridiculing the works was contradicted by a friend, "And in no time," Renoir said, "two rival factions sprang up and came to blows. The police were called, passers-by rushed in from the street, the Hotel Drouot was invaded, absolute mayhem. The doors had to be shut until peace could be restored." It was of enormous help to the struggling young painters.

Before the first World War a French habitué of the Hotel Drouot wrote that the atmosphere was thick with dust and heavy with a foul stale odor, a condition that existed, apparently, until the place was done over in 1969. There is also a legend that dealers engage disagreeable, smelly characters to stand next to outside bidders, until they retreat from the auction room.

The less expensive sales are held downstairs, where the novice would probably be better off to try his luck at first, despite the dust and "garlic-flavored coughing." The rooms downstairs are filled with such as "refrigerators, wicker baskets of books or linen, radios, lesser works of art, all sold without benefit of catalogue or guarantee. Small time dealers and street-market sellers clamor around the auctioneers for bargains, while others sit on top of wardrobes and chests to get a better view."

Upstairs prices are higher and the goods being auctioned are better, the dealers are not quite so rude and the buyers are often polite.

An official of the Hotel Drouot says, "The average French seller prefers to remain anonymous because he is afraid his neighbors will think he needs the money. When an important collection of the property of a famous person is for sale, prices rise 10 to 40 percent." The French are partial to their own 18th century furniture and silver, but many 19th and 20th century items go for a song by comparison. Since there's an enormous quantity of goods on view, some of it is bound to be over-looked, even by the regulars, which makes it possible to get quality at bargain prices. (Don't be surprised if you go to the Paris flea market on Sunday and see some of the same things you saw sold at the Hotel Drouot now on the stalls selling for about ten times what they were bought for at the auction.

Language can present a difficulty at the auction, which is where the commissionaire comes in. He'll tell you whether what you have your eye on is an antique or a reproduction, and its approximate value. He'll also bid for you—just tell him your ceiling bid and tip him two or three francs. You'll know you have your object when the auctioneer says "adjugé" or "vendu" (sold).

There is a tax on everything bought, almost pro-hibitive—16 percent up to 6000 francs, around 11 percent over that. But the French consider that the bargains available, the legal guarantees that go with them, and the richness of the material are sufficient to overcome that barrier.

There are other auctions in France, too—every Sunday afternoon (the day the Hotel Drouot is closed) in the elegant salons at Versailles, where the international ultra-chic set enjoy outbidding each other for often run-of-the-mill objects and paintings and where auctioneers talk of l'amour and make jokes.

Elsewhere

Christie's of London has a Rome office and a Continental H. Q. in Geneva at the elegant Hotel Richemond. They're not equipped to handle regular sales of large works or furniture, which pose a transportation problem and are, therefore, usually routed to their London auction house. In Geneva they have usually jewelry and porcelain sales and small works of art. The sales are conducted in French, although German, Italian and English are also used, and the last bid in Swiss francs is always repeated in English.

Denmark has one major auction house, but it is one of the most distinguished in Europe. The House of Rasmussen has twelve to fourteen auctions a year (none in July or August), sales of everything under the sun, including one or two of vintage wine. In the spring or autumn they have a major international sale that runs for eight to ten days. "Our auctioneering style probably falls somewhere between the English system—where the lot number is given and not much more—and the French system, where there is a great deal of talking on the part of the auctioneer." Sales are conducted in Danish and English with a sprinkling of other languages thrown in. You might see the Danish royal family at Rasmussen's, along with other Danes and an international clientele.

The auctioneer makes an announcement about a colleague
who "grabbed one of those old lamps that need rewiring;
the microphone is a conductor, see, it's not grounded. That
lamp shorted. Almost electrocuted him. They gave him mouth
to mouth and he's in the hospital. Don't know if there's brain
damage."

The auction house collects some commission from the consignor, but the buyer must also pay a 12½ percent commission on top of purchase price. There is an additional 15 percent government purchase tax which can be avoided by foreign buyers when they clear their purchases through a Rasmussen forwarding agent.

There are a number of Swiss auction houses in that small country, as in Bern and Lucerne. Sotheby's chose Zurich for the season's most important jewel auction, instead of New York or London, saying it was more accessible to European buyers and that Americans are more prone to travel. There were skeptical guesses on other reasons, no sales tax in Zurich and the floating dollar among them.

Sotheby's, which has offices in 12 countries, also holds fall and spring sales in Toronto, Canada, and Florence, Italy. Italian auctions, however, are just getting started, confined at present to isolated events, except for PIA and, in Milan, the Finarte. "The best chance for the foreigner to do well lies probably in the field of paintings and drawings. There are still masterpieces of the Renaissance for which, if unsigned, you are almost certain to get an export license."

Although London is considered the center, with a season that runs from October until August, auction houses are found all over Europe (and the Orient too for that matter — recently Christie's became the first foreign auction firm to hold a major sale in Japan). You will find auction houses in Amsterdam and Cologne and Vienna and Munich and Stockholm and Copenhagen, and they all operate pretty much the same way.

If you'll have to bid in a foreign language, you'd be better off to engage a translator or, for large purchases, enlist the services of a dealer.

More pieces of 18th century French furniture are said to have been shipped to New York in one year than could have been made in the whole 18th century.

Imitating old furniture goes back a long time in Europe. Cabinet-makers of the 18th century imitated furniture of the 17th century, and the artisans of Paris were busy for years after the Revolution remaking pieces of every period that had been destroyed. The director of the police laboratory of Paris said, "Everything is subject to falsification—there are even fake Egyptian mummies and fake butterfly collections." The French say *bons chats, bons rats*. That means don't pay any more for anything than it's worth to you as it stands.

Some say that it's better, especially in England, to leave your order-bid with the auctioneer himself, not with an employee, partly because the employee charges a percentage (in England) and the auctioneer charges nothing.

Watch the antiques. It is said that in Italy fakers play enchanting games, and they're good losers when they have to give you your money back.

Spain plays a different variation of the Italian game, but not with the Italian finesse. The subtlety is missing and só is the good humor. "However, they excel in reproducing the implements of their past, which they usually forget to point out as different from other models in age."

164

Watch out for the lead content in any vessel you buy, especially pewter. The U.S. requires that all pewter which might be used for eating purposes, whether domestic or imported, be free of lead, but Europe has no such restriction.

If you bring back a "real antique" from your trip abroad, guaranteed by your receipt to be over 100 years old, and the U.S. Customs tells you it's really a copy, you're going to get stuck for the duty on it—the amount you'd have to pay on a new one. Customs inspectors aren't infallible (if they were, what a great source of authentification!) but they are the on-the-spot judges of what is real and what is fake, and they're pretty good at it.

The Intercourse Flea Market, has auctions too, and one fellow who's been auctioneering there for years is fond of saying he's never found a flea yet.

What something is worth is what it's worth to the buyer. Sometimes the value is almost unlimited, because he wants it; he might spend two or three times an item's value because it fits into his collection and he must have just that.

9

$

There is no arbitrary price set on an object at auction, the price is unique. It seeks its own level, based on supply and demand, and on the competition in each transaction. When the auctioneer has 600 items to put on the block in a sale, he doesn't care if he gets less on this and more on that—it's the aggregate that counts. It's not like a merchant's markup of 600 items that have to make a merchant's markup on each. As one of the New England country auctioneers says, "Can't run an auction and make a profit on every item. People sit at an auction for one reason—they want to get a buy."

Everybody cries about rising auction prices, but the dealers weep the loudest. They all have the same refrain: "There's nothing to get any more, prices are ridiculously high!" or, "Can't go to the auctions any more, the prices are all run up by dudes." I find the same complaint was recorded in 1870, and yearly ever since.

How much?

"If you buy at auction there are no returns, no charge accounts, you pay cash—therefore you should buy at half of retail or less," says one auctioneer.

Price guides are published every year, available at most libraries, which take their information from all over the country and average it out. The prices are based on "proof pieces" (objects without defects) and 10 percent to 20 percent has to be allowed for regional differences. ("'Plantation made' is big in the South," says an auctioneer, "and Empire you can't give away up north but it goes at Southern sales like crazy. Foreign antiques, which are usually of darker wood than American, have greater appeal in the South; the lighter wood goes better out West.")

There is still a great deal of fluctuation. Prices might run quite high because something has been out of circulation for a long time and there weren't many opportunities to get one. Then if several of them appear on the market at the same time, it waters down the demand and shoots down the price.

A thing in itself has no intrinsic value. The value is set by the people who want it. When a lot of people started to collect pre-Columbian sculpture, for instance, terra-cotta vessels in the shape of hairless dogs (which were raised for food) were very popular at auctions. After a while the collectors shifted their interest to more sophisticated Mayan and Olmec objects, and the prices of the folksy sculptures went down to one-third or one-half of what was paid ten to fifteen years ago.

The price can even depend on who's at the auction that day. If no one there wants the object, it goes for nothing. If two rich men want it there's no limit to its price. There was a famous 11th century Royal Chinese vase auctioned in London which two rich men both wanted. They bid up to the largest price ever paid for such an object—the auctioneer said he normally would have guessed it would go for one-tenth the amount it brought.

A New York auctioneer says, "I have seen a lithograph sold for $85 and the identical same object, in just as good condition, with a larger and more complex audience, go for $800." The auction-goer's dream is to be part of that small, non-competitive audience and get the Great Buy.

Natural pearls are one of the few jewels that have markedly dropped in value over the years, but the La Peregrina pearl, which was once part of the Spanish crown jewels, was valuable to Elizabeth Taylor, who bought it—maybe for its romantic associations.

Americana has been steadily rising in price—with one exception: American silver, which has not kept the pace of Americana in other fields.

Pewter was in much demand in the 1920s and then it fell from favor for a long time. It is just now coming back with prices higher than ever. One auctioneer says that the demand for Americana is so great and the supply so limited people are buying anything—light pole insulators, fresca bottles. And they might get stuck with them. "Paintings and certain heavy furniture that sold in the 1880s for thousands of dollars now bring in nickels in comparison because nobody wants them now."

Fads are strange things that just creep in, nobody knows from where. When they arrive, up go prices, because suddenly there's a short supply. A Boston auctioneer knows that "regardless of how good something is or how fine or how old, everything is based on fads and fashions. Take, for example, a 1550 French walnut court cupboard sold by French and Company in the 1920s for $12,000. It couldn't be reproduced for $5000, and they couldn't get $500 for it today. It's archaic, tremendous in size, baronial. But in the 1920s there was a willing buyer for $12,000 from a willing seller.''

Value and bargains

"Bargains?" says a British cynic. "Instead of getting something for nothing, you are more likely to get nothing for something." But a western auctioneer looks at it differently. "Remember that no two people put the same valuation on an item. If you've bought something at an auction, don't tear your hair wondering if you've made a good buy. Relax and enjoy it." His Eastern counterpart says, "Whether everything you bring home is a bargain or not doesn't matter. If you like it, you have a bargain."

An old down-easter warns that you can get fooled on bargains, so unless you know exactly what you're doing, (here it comes again) buy only what you like, to have and enjoy. Example A: you have a picture by Smith Jones and have searched for years and couldn't find any record of its being sold at auction. Therefore, it must be valuable because rare, and if you see another one at auction, you'll bid big on it, right? Wrong. Auction annuals make no record of pictures sold under $100.

Example B: You read in a newspaper about a document signed by a historic person sold for a

large sum of money. You catch sight of a document
with a similar signature at auction that you can get
for one-third the figure you saw in the newspaper.
Great Bargain, right? Wrong. The price depends not
only on the signature but also on the importance of
the document.

C: You see a whole library up for auction in some
out-of-the-way place, and the bidding is slow
and you can get this library for next to nothing.
You're stealing a march on some unknowing hicks,
right? Maybe—If you have inspected the library and
find something like half a dozen copies of the
American Almanac that are worth more than all the
rest of the books put together.

Attributes that do not make an object valuable:
"You can see it's old!" or "It's handmade!" or
"It must be over a hundred years old!" or "It's
handpainted and signed!" When some self-appointed
expert tells you it must be worth at least so much,
ask him to buy it for that. What constitutes value?
If you cherish old junk and want to bid on it, fine.
But don't forget that as far as the expert is concerned, it's junk. Lots of people treasure nondescript
china, old books, furniture, pewter or Sheffield
ware, but the china is not rare or artistic; the
books, though old, are valueless because they are
reprint editions; the furniture is all wrong in style
and construction; the pewter is not pewter at all but
Britannia; the Sheffield isn't Sheffield (copper and
silver sheets annealed and solidified) but simple
copper with a thin electroplate.

Value is not only quality, it's also a matter of rarity.
For instance, the $5 gold piece dated 1822, ac-
cording to the government, was worth basically $5.
It is actually worth many thousands of dollars,

because that is what collectors of old coins will pay for it. If it were a four-drachma piece (60¢) of the time of Alexander the Great (300 B.C.) it would sell for a few hundred at most, because it is easier to find than the 1822 gold piece.

A fellow up Vermont way says, "Take court cupboards, one of the earliest pieces of furniture for American homes. In appearance it faintly resembles the offspring of a clumsy sideboard that enjoyed an affair of the heart with an old-fashioned telephone booth or a New England outhouse. It is not, in short, a particularly beautiful piece of furniture, but since most of the early court cupboards were broken up for firewood long ago, an undamaged specimen is rarely encountered and so is held in very high esteem."

The value of matched things changes the value of one of them. For instance, a set of six chairs will be bid higher than the sum of each chair sold separately. Where a single candlestick might sell for $20, a pair of the same pattern could bring $100. If you have a single fine object, and see at an auction its exact match, you'll probably be able to buy the matching object for a small price and at the same time increase the value of the two together by 300 percent to 500 percent.

What something is worth is what it's worth to the buyer. Sometimes the value is almost unlimited, because he wants it; he might spend two or three times an item's value because it fits into his collection and he must have just that. A shrewd country auctioneer says, "Top dollar is paid by the man who comes to buy one thing. He can be led and swayed and pushed." A buyer who is just as shrewd says, "To enjoy what you buy, first you

172

. . . dealers frequently have a grudge against an auctioneer, so go to more than one person for advice.''

have to pay for it only an amount of money that is not going to make a worm gnaw you each time you look at it."

Or take the value of a cedar chest to this New Hampshire women: She bought a clock for $800 and then bought a cedar chest to put the clock in so her husband wouldn't see it.

Good buys

"Buy now," says the auctioneer, "only the very best of anything. Junk is tough to get rid of in hard times but there's a buyer for everything good, no matter what the times. "And," he adds, "junk always costs more money, comparatively. The higher the price, the better buy you get. You can never steal a cheap item, but you can a fine one."

The Vice President of Parke-Bernet told me that prices of antique furniture and objets d'art rose by 100 to 200 percent in the sixties. "American and French furniture, even 19th century copies of earlier pieces, have gone up *at least* 200 percent in the last decade. English furniture hasn't risen so fast, although it will match the other in a few years.

"People don't buy monstrosities any more just because they're old. Good American Victorian furniture goes for reasonably good prices, but very few people, now or ever, will buy the ugly or over-ornate, ponderous things. I don't see how early 19th century New England simple country furniture can help but go up in price and even the sophisti-cated pieces that have been in demand since 1928."

An unknown or unsung maker of anything may be famous tomorrow; witness the Tiffany lamps that were selling from $3 to $5 in the 1950s, and have risen right up out of sight.

Parke-Bernet points out that jewelry, including very modestly priced pieces, is often sold at auction for lower prices than it can be bought for otherwise. "We know many times what someone pays the jeweler, and we know it was more than we got for it. Dealers buy here too, and they're not buying unless they can make a profit."

Art works have their own peculiar set of values, among them size. Although the occasional grotesque hugeness of some abstract paintings hasn't seemed to affect their price, older masters bring depressed prices when they're too large. Most tapestries are a drug on the market for the same reason. "Fish, no matter how beautifully painted, are harder to sell than flowers, and portrait paintings sell by the rule of 'women and children first'. The presence of a skull, a skeleton or blood of any kind cuts the price down severely, which explains why such details are often painted out."

We always have to come back to the worth of a name in art, and conclude that the price of the work hasn't much to do with its artistic merit. There was the much publicized case of the Frick Collection, which acquired for a considerable sum a painting attributed to Jacques-Louis David. Not too long ago research established that the picture was actually painted by a totally unknown French lady. "If the picture had been marketed under the name of its true author, it would have fetched a very small fraction of the price paid for it as a David. Yet it was still the same picture and a very fine one indeed. The price difference was solely due to a mix-up of labels."

Investing

There's an old joke among dealers about the man who comes into the gallery and says, "Show me some growth paintings."

The Vice President of Parke-Bernet Auction Galleries told me in the mid-1960s "With inflation, people often tend to put their capital into real goods today. Europeans have been doing it for centuries — you can put jewelry into your pocket, or take a picture and go anywhere with it. Americans have begun to look for security by putting not just income but capital into art works and fine goods."

Even a small town auctioneer says, "Nowadays the majority are acutely value conscious, seeking some bulwark against continuing inflation." The man who owns the only Gutenberg Bible in private hands puts it this way: "I'm not very eager to sell, because I will never in my life have another Gutenberg Bible. If I had, say, the two or two-and-a-half million dollars it's worth invested even in tax-exempt bonds, I'd be losing money because of inflation. So, as an investor I like to keep this type of material because it gets more and more valuable. If inflation goes on like it is, in ten years I will still be all right."

The question is, of course, will inflation and the economy continue to go up? An old-time dealer points out, "Antiques and works of art are really worthwhile investments — you can turn them into cash just as you can stocks and bonds, but if there's a shortage of money, people are not inclined to buy luxuries, just necessities. Great rarities can bring fantastic prices, but in the 1920s people thought that and in the '30s they had to give them away." Still, an economist says, "Since well before 1900 prices of old things have risen and risen and

176

risen—sometimes with a peak, it's true—but the graph line has only moved permanently in the direction of up."

Investment in fine goods, the expert feels, generally takes the form of a triangle—security, marketability, and yield. "Security would mean only good authentic pieces in proof condition—nothing that is reproduced or of which there is any question. For long-term investment value, it has to be the best that money can buy, oddities and rarities being the exceptions to that rule, especially where their history makes them important."

Value might always be present in an object, but not always marketability, because popularity waxes and wanes. Marketability means you can't always sell something just when you want to. It also means that if you're shrewd and lucky you might pick up at auction, for just a small part of its value, an item that is momentarily out of favor.

Yield means the actual profit you make when you sell. You might be able to sell something you picked up years ago for twenty or fifty times what you paid for it. But to find your true yield, first you'd have to compare dollar value then and now, and that means you'd have to write off considerable paper profit right there. Then, since you'd have had to hang on to the item for many years, you'd have to figure what the dollars would have brought you invested at compound interest.

Money invested at six percent compound interest will double itself in twelve years. It's possible that antiques, for one thing, can double in half that time, and with that possibility there's always the enjoyment of beautiful things that doesn't come with money in the bank or pieces of real estate.

Maybe the investment is "money of no real consequence," peanuts, like buying something for $25 and finding in a few years it's worth $50. Well, why shouldn't you invest in a modest way and make money in a modest way? Objects of solid worth will always pay dividends.

What experts say to invest in

There are a few general fields most people choose for investment, although the specialties within those categories would probably go several times around a roll of adding machine paper.

Antiques

Amy Vanderbilt, for one, feels that antiques are like money in the bank. "Stocks can be manipulated, old things cannot. Some antiques go up slowly, some at incredible speed, but all go up."

Antiques in pristine condition command higher and higher prices. One collector makes plain what he thinks of any kind of antiques: "Humbler folk with less money who love the past may be quite as happy with pieces in something less than perfect condition, and enjoy fully as great a personal satisfaction, without investment intention." To us humbler folk a country auctioneer says, "I'll give you a tip: pick up any piece of furniture that has a concave mirror, and chances are you've found a real old-time item that is probably worth a good bit."

The president of a mutual fund says he's discovered that his prized American furniture is appreciating as fast as the investments he had made for the fund. In a few years certain important pieces have increased three and four times in value, although authentic but not particularly important things have not gone up anywhere near such a degree.

Many investors think furnishings are the most solid investment because of the economics of faking, as opposed to such collectors' items as campaign ribbons, metal candle molds, buttons, etc.

"If I knew twenty-five years ago what I know today," laments an auctioneer, "and put it into antique furniture, I would have been a millionaire several times over. If twenty-five years ago a person had bought French and English and American furniture, and Fabergé Russian enamels, and jade, and Impressionist paintings, this man would have been 400 times ahead of investing in the stock market."

Experts, who know how to tell the real from the fake, say good antique silver keeps going up in price, and that despite a momentarily depressed market, silver as bullion keeps reaching record prices per ounce in the world market, "so many people who care little for fine silver for itself are attracted to old silver as an investment. It is inconceivable that anyone today paying a sensible price for fine pieces of antique silver will not see a gain on their outlay. Some prices have doubled in a couple of years, so as a short term investment it can be worthwhile. Besides which, silver is a portable asset that may be liquidated at any time." Certain investors recommend Continental silver as less expensive than English silver's inflated prices and a better hedge against any devaluation and inflation.

Old copper and brass often appear at auction for quite reasonable prices, in all kinds of objects and

While the demand for the best wines has grown enormously, there is very little capability for increasing their production much, and that's what had led to investing and speculating in the growths.

curios, some of them even excavated from ancient sites. But of course, this field is also mined by fakers, so you have to be very careful.

Antique porcelain and ceramics—undamaged—can still take a modest investment and show a return.

Some of the biggest gains are reported at the low end of the market. One professional says the kind of miscellaneous plate or undistinguished chair that brought fifty cents in a country auction a few years ago, now goes for $5 to $10. In his opinion, "The man with great rarities and the man with junk are way ahead of the game, while the safe middle roader is losing out to inflationary tendencies."

"Victoriana!" is the advice of another experienced counselor, "The best you can afford, and it promises to produce a better return one day than your stock or bond investments." He bases this judgment on the fact that it happened with Regency furnishings, and "judging by the rapid upward trend of prices, it will be repeated with Victoriana." Victorian objects are plentiful, after years of neglect and derision, which were partly deserved, since it was often imitative and gaudy, even "tawdry and repellant." However, there was also much that was inventive, curious, amusing, quaint, and even beautiful objects of lasting attraction.

The 19th century was an experimental age and it is the novelty of experimentation that should be considered, which doesn't necessarily mean horse-chair sofas and tables made of antlers.

The Victorian period lasted so long that time itself helped in the proliferation of everything from monstrosities to inventive curiosities. Because much of it still survives there is a unique opportunity to buy for modest sums. Until now one advantage of speculating in Victoriana was that it hasn't been considered worth faking, and is very likely to be genuine, but popularity will no doubt bring the reproductions out in full blossom.

Wines

Investors in wines say for most economic buying they have to be purchased when young, within six months or so of vintage. "About six or seven years after the vintage, a successfully chosen wine may well become many times more valuable, how much depending on the rarity and demand." While the demand for the best wines has grown enormously, there is very little capability for increasing their production much, and that's what has led to investing and speculating in the growths.

Autographs

Among the vintage cars, prints, rare books, coins, art works, etc. that more and more professionals have been speculating in for profit, a popular entry has been autographs and documents signed by famous people. They've been spiraling up and up over the years, beating more traditional investments by giant steps. It goes without saying that you either have to know what you're doing, or get the advice of someone who does.

The importance of the documents has an effect on its value, but rarity also sets a price on famous names. For instance, Stalin's signature is so rare, even a menu signed by him brings thousands of dollars. By contrast, documents signed by Napoleon

are hardly worth $100, because he signed a total
of a half a million papers. Autographs by movie
stars don't have any special value (with a few
exceptions like Greta Garbo, W. C. Fields, Rudolf
Valentino) because there are just too many of them
around.

Art

Art appreciation used to mean aesthetic enjoyment
of art. Now it means propensity to rise in price.
Works of art aren't considered just something to hang
on the wall any more — they're investments, like
stock, and we are told we can bank on that.
Inflation is always cited as one reason, and several
years before the dollar was devalued the newspapers
wrote about a lot of Americans who were beginning
to distrust the dollar and tie their money up in art.
Europeans were also speculating to protect themselves against possible devaluation of the pound,
the franc, and other currencies.

In periods of inflation and widespread uneasiness
about money, people of wealth tend to put their
money into commodities least affected by the
economic weather. The uniqueness of art objects
has made them a durable investment.

Not all art prices inevitably go up, even though
experts expect American art to increase in price
from 50 percent to 100 percent by 1975, and then
go higher as the nation enters its Bicentennial year.
(Too bad the artists rarely benefit).

When Dow-Jones averages drop, say the sachems,
investors would rather gamble on Corot's future
than corn futures. They also warn that it's just as
tricky a speculation, for paintings often depreciate in

value even more rapidly than they increase. That sour note out of the way, they add that the official price reports show that a good American painting sold in 1960 for about four times what it sold for in 1950, and in 1970 it sold for almost twenty times its 1950 price.

There's more interest now in prints than ever before, and that, of course, has made the prices go up. "In the next few years," says a professional, "prices in the print market will keep rising, but selectively. There will be a weeding out of certain mediocre Picassos and Miros, for instance." Another one says, "Prices in the print market are still rising, especially in my field (German Expressionists and Bauhaus Graphics) as compared to Picasso, whose prices are leveling off."

We are advised not to buy prints with the idea of a *quick* investment, and cautioned, when buying prints as an investment, to buy individual prints rather than sets, checking the condition very carefully, of course.

Tip

If someone hasn't done too well in stocks, he could try cornflakes, the ones with the pictures of baseball players in the boxes. Guaranteed 20 percent profit if you have what other such card collectors need. But caution is advised: One midwestern collector's wife sued for divorce after her husband began buying cornflakes by the case to get the cards—having to make cornflake stew and cornflake pie and conflake soup constituted cruel and abusive treatment. (There is also a market for bubblegum cards and possibly for pictures of the ballplayers on Milk Duds.)

184

That ol' black magic, demand

The time factor is the essence. If you buy when
everyone else wants the same thing, you have
much less chance of getting a bargain. Wise buying
comes, usually, before or after the general public,
for demand is the base for the rise or fall of prices.
If no one wants a particular thing, then it is valueless as far as selling it is concerned.

Item: Alma-Tadema's "Finding of Moses" brought
$25,000 in 1904 (when the dollar was worth at least
three times what it is today), and was sold in 1960
for about $700. Price deflation can also occur in
shorter periods. A painting by Maris that went for
$15,000 in 1924 brought $400 eight years later; a
Toulouse-Lautrec from the Somerset Maugham
collection auctioned in 1966 brought only 40 percent of the price Maugham paid for it at auction
in 1962. In 1949 a Rosa Bonheur herd of bulls
fetched one-third what it had been bought at with
1887 dollars. Bonheurs today are going up again,
but as with any investment, the question is how
much and how long you have to wait.

Nineteenth century artists, who had once been
"inscribed in the golden book of immortality"
became the forgotten men of the art market after the
battle for Impressionism had been won. "The
advent of new artistic currents has frequently been
the cause of the downfall of the old gods, and it
would be foolish to think that today's champions
will be exempt from such a fate. Only time will tell
which artists and movements will be hit the hardest"
— and, he should have added, which investors.

There are some companies, like one based in
Lichtenstein called Artemis (the huntress goddess),

which buy works of art purely as an investment, like blue-chip stocks. They pursue mainly "safe" art (the biggest names) and it is reputed that what they buy is stored in vaults and never sees the light of day.

Rare book dealers used to be the ones accused of uniquely collecting for financial gain. It may be considered a disgrace by book lovers, but investors are admiring of the figures: up an average of 50 percent every year for the last several. "If books are important and in good condition, they'll always hold up. They're blue chips. If you've bought wisely, they'll appreciate enough to beat inflation." But— always that but—it is also possible to take a bath in the rare book market too. "It has its trends just like any other field, and sometimes the trends are just a case of sheep following sheep. In the 1920s first editions of some Bernard Shaw works cost about $350—today they go for about $50; Galsworthy prices went into the thousands then—$100 would be a common price now."

An important auctioneer cites: "Take the case of Georgian silver—some of the finest examples the world has ever seen, are also the worst for investment purposes. Right now the Georgian silver market is way off from two years ago, due to inflation. People with free money bought without regard to price, then when money's tight, there aren't any buyers at those prices, let alone bigger ones."

Huge prices were paid in the 1880s for majolica ware, enamels, objects in precious materials, many of which were rejected by the collectors before the turn of the century, becoming unsaleable, the equivalent of worthless for an investor. Then in the

"It's harder to sell a genuine painting."
Rubens painted 2000 pictures, of which 5000
are in the United States.

1960s there was a considerable recovery, but "it has been slow, fitful and nothing like total."

The investing bewares

The professional keeps saying it: The only time to buy for investment is when you know absolutely what you're doing. Otherwise, buy ONLY FOR PLEASURE—there is very little reason to buy anything you don't like.

1. Beware the pitfall of Who Done It

A well-known London dealer says "Quality should be the touchstone. However much prestige may accrue to the owner of a scrap by a fashionable name, it is not likely to compensate for its low rating in investment value. The finest example by a minor artist is preferable to a poor or damaged picture by a big name, for it is the good things which have the elasticity in value which will reward the investor in the long run."

The foremost authority on precious rugs says, "They are to be judged primarily by their intrinsic beauty. They are created for the purpose of being beautiful. Rarity, historical association and fashion are generally irrelevant. The alert and discerning few who have the independence of judgment to buy things on the basis of sheer beauty can reap a great harvest."

2. Beware the 'burned' work of art.

There's a mysterious chemistry in auctions of fine things which decrees that when a work fails to meet its reserve it sometimes becomes tainted. When that happens, a veteran notes, the auctioneer may

188

contact the next highest bidder to ask if he'll take it, and "you'd be surprised how often that man will say 'I don't want it any longer.'" (That's a case in point where a reserve hurts the work it was meant to protect).

3. Beware of holding on too long if you expect to make a profit in a rising market.

Demand can send prices beyond the reach of average auction-goers, whereupon they often shift their attention suddenly to something else.

4. Beware to remember that condition governs all prices.

If one piece of a pair or set is damaged, it reduces the value of the remaining piece. (A pair, like a salt and pepper, is always worth more than twice the price of each piece singly.)

A tiny mark, or a flaw such as a slight fire crack, which may seem inconsequential, makes a great difference in the value between two apparently identical pieces. It's true that you can see cracked pieces in museum collections, but only something extraordinarily fine or rare will hold up in value with a damage or a mend.

5. Beware not to be misled by institution-sponsored auctions.

When an upstate New York Institute of Art held an auction to raise money, the museum itself put in some items, for they had more than they needed of certain things, but the majority were donated by the people of the city. "People were buying at prices three and four times reasonable worth," says an auctioneer, "they should have asked in advance instead of assuming that because the museum had its name on the auction these things were museum quality. There were no bargains up there except a few very fine things that most people didn't appreciate. The dealers had a ball."

6. Beware not to throw out the baby with the bathwater.

Toleware (painted sheet iron popular in the middle of the 19th century), for instance, depends on the condition of its decoration. A piece from about 1860 may be worth, say, $50 if the decoration is excellent, $35 if the decoration is worth preserving, and $15 if the decoration is ruined (in which case you'd be better off to sand it down and re-do it).

7. Beware of paying for a phony label.

The presence of copies of old labels printed on torn-out fly leaves of old books can increase the value of a legitimate antique by a couple of hundred dollars.

8. Beware of the "bargain" antique.

"A curly maple butterfly table that goes for $200 or $300 means the auctioneer is a fool, a crook, or an innocent stooge for a faker." The original caveat emptor: "Such bargains don't exist because they don't need to exist."

9. Beware of "bargain" art, especially American primitives.

The fakes expert says forging has become such lucrative business in Europe that certain towns are known for their specialties, like those who make Innesses, or the ones who make Corots, or Van Goghs. There's even a school for them in one Belgian town. "The whole point is just to remind you not to buy any of these bargains beyond what it is worth to you to own reproductions. The investment value is nil."

In 1918 a famous French dealer wrote in his diary, "A fake Gainsborough, a "Blue Boy," has just been knocked down in New York for $32,000. It's harder to sell a genuine painting." Rubens painted 2000 pictures, of which 5000 are in the United States. Twenty-eight thousand paintings by Corot are sworn to be in existence, which means he completed 1½ paintings every day of his painting life, including Sundays and holidays.

The true auction-goer knows that if money is no object, it's no trick to outbid everybody else and buy something at a crazy price. But the point is, what sport is there in that kind of buying? He might as well go out and shoot sitting ducks or dynamite a few fish. Auctions aren't just how big a check someone can write—they're the joy of the chase, of discovering something yourself, they're the suspense . . . and the triumph!

ACKNOWLEDGMENTS

Mr. and Mrs. Robert C. Eldred, East Dennis, Mass.;
Mr. Harold R. Pick, Winnetka, Ill.; Miss Mary
Vandegrift, New York City; Mr. Milton Lubar, Boston;
Mr. Richard A. Bourne, Hyannis; Mr. A. Hanzel,
Chicago; Mr. Liebson and Mrs. Birnbaum, New
York; Mr. John J. McGrath, Jr., Boston; Mr. William
O'Reilly, New York; Mr. Hamilton Osgood,
Cambridge; Mr. William Kranzler, New Bedford.

Also Mrs. Louis Joseph, Boston; Mr. George
Considine, South Dartmouth; Mr. Andrew Rubin,
Hollywood, Calif.; Mr. Raymond Woodhouse, North
Dartmouth, Mass.; Mr. Richard Norton, Chicago;
Mr. Louis Cardoza, Fairhaven, Mass.; Mr. Richard
Rubin, Westport, Conn.; Mrs. I. G. Fox, Bal
Harbour, Fla.; Mr. and Mrs. Henry Winogrond,
Brattleboro, Vermont.

And Mrs. L. Warling and Miss V. Goddard of Los
Angeles; Miss M. Barton, San Francisco; Mr. Dennis
Broadbent, New Bedford; Mrs. Helen Loring,
Atlanta, Georgia; Mrs. Helene Robecheck, Chicago;
Mr. J. Ussiker, New York.